In the name of God, the beneficent, the merciful

Mysterious Seyyid and his Students

Inspirational stories for those who wish to taste righteousness...

Ghulam Habib

Author: Ghulam Habib
Publisher: Jerrmein AbuShaba
ISBN-10: 1733028404
ISBN-13: 978-1733028400
Year: 2019

Dedicated to the divine spirit of

Imam Khomeini (ra)

the great teacher of ethics and mysticism who inspired millions

Contents

Foreword by the Author

Stories provide a better means of communicating ideas than simple text without examples. This is also the Qur'anic style of teaching divine values and high human qualities. I was inspired by Martyr Bint al Huda Sadr (r) to write the stories for the present book.

The stories presented in this small book illustrate a human role model in the form of a spiritual teacher 'Seyyid', who provides spiritual and ethical guidance and inspiration and affects the life of several young students and people who attend his lectures. His lectures focus on common ethical and ideological topics that are suited to the needs of young students. He also practically guides students and helps people. Different ways to carry out a sincere action is the main message of these stories.

It is hoped that these stories will be useful for the instructors of ethics and for Sunday schools as well as for the college and university students.

Ghulam Habib[1]
2015

---

1 Pen name of author

Birr and Abrar

لَنْ تَنَالُوا الْبِرَّ حَتَّىٰ تُنْفِقُوا مِمَّا تُحِبُّونَ ۚ وَمَا تُنْفِقُوا مِنْ شَيْءٍ فَإِنَّ اللَّهَ بِهِ عَلِيمٌ

By no means shall you attain to righteousness until you spend (benevolently) out of what you love; and whatever thing you spend, Allah surely knows it.

[Qur'an, 3:92]

It was the usual gathering on Saturday evening after *maghrib* and *'isha* prayers in the yard of Seyyid's house and he began his lecture with the recitation of above verse of Qur'an to the limited audience….

He began: 'The word '*birr*' in Arabic has many meanings, all pointing towards righteous deed. Every good deed doesn't fall into the category of '*birr*' or righteous deed. Many human beings do good deeds; however, either because of their intention or the circumstances in which the good deed was done or their words, gestures or actions after doing that deed, it is excluded from being '*birr*'. In the Holy Qur'an, this word is used in different contexts, all of which point to high quality good deeds for the sake of God. The person who is pious is called '*barr*' in Arabic and its plural is '*abrar*', those who do pious deeds and they have a very high place in heaven. The verse I have recited points to many deeper aspects of human life and the way human beings live and treat each other. Under normal circumstances, human beings usually help each other because it's the human nature and God has created human beings as such. It is also the custom or norm of a society or people of a locality or members of a family or a group or close friends to help each other and provide support in difficult times. Most of the times, it is a give and take relationship. However, doing a righteous action [*birr*] only for the sake of God is really very difficult, if not impossible, because it is not based on a give and take good done usually.

The prime criterion set by the Holy Qur'an for achieving '*birr*' is that one has to spend or give something in the way of God that is very valuable, something that is highly loved by a person or towards which a person has very much emotional attachment or one is in need of it at the time of giving it in the way of God. It doesn't mean only money or valuable material possession; it can be other things also such as one's own normal peaceful life, one's daily routine, one's family, one's valuable time, expertise, social prestige, career, and other highly valuable and dear things that one loves more dearly than any other thing.

Secondly, one should not expect anything in return, not even thanks for the good action. One should consider it only a duty carried out for the sake of God's pleasure. One should try to do the good action before the person in need asks for it. This means that one should be aware of those near him and be quick and also search for those in need so that timely help and support can be offered at the right time and to protect self-respect of a person who doesn't like to ask for help. One should make utmost effort to preserve it, keep it a secret until death and protect it from ostentation (*riya*). Finally, one should be thankful and pray for the person to whom he has done good because it was due to him that he was able to do the righteous action.'

He continued.... 'Most of the times good actions are done but the intentions are not clear. Sometimes, because a person likes to do it or it is his habit, while at other times, it is out of external force or pressure such as to save one's prestige or to show one's generosity or to preserve one's social status. Sometimes, it is out of strong emotional feeling while at other times, it is due to a feeling of escape out of anxiety or depression. Sometimes, the intention is known to the doer and seems good to him, but in reality it is not. Sometimes, the good action is done to make a show of it and gain worldly benefit or profit. And sometimes, the intention is also pure for the sake of God and the action is done for the sake of God. However, after sometime, the person cannot protect the good action and makes show of it, talks about it, hints at it to draw someone's attention, or subtly expresses it indirectly by a bodily gesture and so the action no longer remains in the category of *birr*... It is nullified by ostentation, when God doesn't give reward for it and the meager return for that action then comes from creatures.

Another beauty of good action is to do it under the most difficult circumstances, for example, doing the good action right at the time when it should be done even though a person is very tired, under stress, depressed, or under his own personal difficulties or problems. The more severe the difficulty, the better will be the quality of good action and acceptance by God. Another example is to do good and help someone whom a person doesn't like or someone who has harmed or angered him unjustly. Several examples of such good actions are found in the life of Ahlul Bayt (as). In addition, the good action should be done in such a way so as to not make the person who is helped feel ashamed. It should be done secretly. One should also protect that action while one deals with that person or meets him and should not make show of it which is very difficult.

Best example of *birr* is in the life of Ahlul Bayt (as) when Imam Ali (as), Hazrat Fatima (sa), Imam Hasan (as) and Imam Husayn (as) observed fast for three days and gave away their food to needy persons at the time of *iftar* for those three days. They had no food to eat for three days while they fasted. They didn't inform anyone of this highly noble action of self-sacrifice and worship of God until Prophet (swas) was informed by angel Jibraeel and then verses of Qur'an were revealed in praise of their sincere action for the pleasure of God. God thanked them for their utmost sincere action.....

The reason Qur'an mentions that '*abrar*' are in high place in heavens is perhaps these righteous individuals keep their good deeds hidden and safe from any ostentation, showing off and other such acts that would give a worldly return until their death. However, it doesn't mean that one should not do any good deed openly in a society that is necessary to be done in public or for the sake of rescuing and helping poor or downtrodden people. Here the intention is divine and remains hidden while the deed becomes known to most of the people. Such difficult deeds in this world makes '*abrar*' eligible for divine reward reserved for '*illiyun*'. The best example of such a great personality is Imam Husayn (as) who did the highest good deed of enjoining the right and forbidding the evil against the despotic tyrant of his time, Yazid, to save Islam and sacrificed his life, his own family members and his loyal friends in Karbala under the most difficult circumstances.

I wish you all try to do only one good action for the sake of God, keep it safe until you die and become *abrar,* the righteous ones God has mentioned in this holy verse. You have to be vigilant and careful while doing it. You have to be careful even after doing it. Make a firm will with sincere intention and pray to God for help, He will help you… I will specially ask few of you who are regular and close to me about your experience of a good action after one year… *Insha'Allah…*'

After the lecture, Seyyid sat on the floor as usual with audience and then looked at some of the university students and smiled. Those students included Sobhan, Qamar, Asad, Bilal, Shahid, Yusuf, Shareef, Ahmad, Mostafa, Ibrahim, Vaheed and Husayn who were very close to him and were among his regular audience. They were from different family and social backgrounds. Several other people were also present and Seyyid's house was always open for anyone seeking advice on different issues.

People then started asking him their questions and seeking his guidance on various personal matters. It was the weekly *tafsir* of Qur'an lecture on Saturday evening after *maghrib* prayers. The students close to Seyyid who were very good friends were now seriously discussing how to taste the righteous action according to the criteria explained by Seyyid. They moved a bit away from where Seyyid was sitting with others so that they could discuss in private. A few minutes later, the dinner was being served but their discussion was continuing. Ahmad said that he has recorded Seyyid's lecture and will email the important points to them. After dinner they went near Seyyid requesting him to pray for them to achieve success and said goodbye to him.

Death of Father

Two weeks later, Qamar's father passed away. Seyyid went to his house for condolences and then sat with him. He was the eldest son. His family was rich and had business, both inside the country and abroad. Two of his brothers were abroad, studying in universities. Qamar now lived with one sister and his mother. The whole family was very religious, humble in behavior and their life style was very moderate.

Qamar was a regular attendee of Seyyid's lectures and was usually very quiet and sober in his manners. His life had changed after meeting Seyyid a few years ago. He would often recall how Seyyid surprised him and changed his way of thinking and his life…

When he met Seyyid for the first time, he was preparing for his bachelor's degree's final exam and somehow accidentally met one of Seyyid's students, Mostafa. Mostafa took him to offer *maghrib* prayers and then unintendedly he attended Seyyid's lecture on 'spiritual pleasure.' He was very much impressed by Seyyid's words. After the lecture, he sat near Seyyid and asked a few questions on spiritual pleasure. Then, he asked Seyyid: 'How can I feel spiritual pleasure?' Seyyid saw a new book in his hands and asked about it. Qamar said that he had just bought this book and that it was the expensive latest edition and that he had a final exam after ten days. 'I am among the top students of my class Seyyid and this book will help me get first position in final exams because I don't think my classmates know about it.' Seyyid smiled and very calmly asked Qamar to photocopy the book and give the original expensive book as a gift to a poor student of his class whom he thinks is able to compete with him in final exams. Qamar didn't believe what he had heard and so he asked: 'What did you say Seyyid?' Seyyid smiled again and said: 'Yes do it.

Tell me what happens to you. And remember, don't tell anyone about it.' Qamar was in a state of shock and then said goodbye to Seyyid. Seyyid prayed for his success.

After his exams were over, Qamar came to Seyyid's house one day at *zuhr* and sat a bit away. Seyyid saw him and after prayers asked him to come closer. Then, Seyyid asked him about his exams. Qamar said that his performance was very good and he was waiting for results. Finally, Seyyid asked him softly: 'Did you do it?' Qamar replied: 'Yes, Seyyid.' 'How do you feel?' Seyyid asked him. 'I cannot describe the joy, the feeling inside that made me as if I am free of all stresses; like total peace inside myself. It was a pleasure that I never had before and it never leaves me whenever I think of it. It is still there Seyyid.' Then Seyyid asked him to pray two *rak'at* prayers to thank God for this opportunity. 'Keep it up Qamar,' said Seyyid.

All the students of Seyyid had one or more such shocking good experiences from Seyyid that changed their lives and made them very close to Seyyid. His noble style of teaching and training them was the reason and very often, these students would bring their friends and family members to Seyyid for guidance.

Every once in a while, Qamar would invite his close friends to his house for gatherings and playing games, share their good experiences, etc. He had passed his MBA shortly before his father died and was now applying for specialized diploma courses to strengthen his knowledge in marketing and other areas for managing his family business which he had inherited from his father.

All the friends were at his house on the 40th day after the death of his father and Seyyid gave a very inspiring lecture on *bala*, or tribulations and hardships in one's life. He explained that *bala* is a necessary ingredient of a believer's life. He said: 'God doesn't test us by placing an exam paper in front of us, like we are tested in our school, college and university. God creates a scenario around us and tests us. The first thing one has to do is to be patient and the second thing is to have trust in God and then one should pray more and do one's best in that situation. The beauty of God's exam is that it is always according to one's level of faith and ability and another characteristic is that He tests us with innovative ways next time – from something we love most, or from something we never thought of before. Everyone's *bala* is according to the level of his faith, nearness to God and his ability. Prophet Muhammad (swas) said that no prophet was tormented to his extent. Imam Ali (as) has praised God for tests with which He examines His servants every time with a new situation. There is a sermon in *Nahjul Balagha* that begins with the praise of God for His new ways of testing his servants,' he continued. Seyyid ended his lecture with few advices about the importance of reading Holy Qur'an: 'I advise young college and university students that they should read Holy Qur'an like their course book, not casually as most of the people read it in their daily life. A student should make habit of reading this divine course book daily. There is divine wisdom in each and every word of Qur'an. One should ponder over the meaning of each and every word in it and find the reason as to why God has used in a particular *ayah*. Holy Qur'an is the ultimate book of science for every human being and its depth never ends. The more we ponder, the more we discover the hidden meanings in it.' All those present listened quietly to Seyyid's words of wisdom and appreciated his practical knowledge about life and interpretation of Islamic traditions.

After everyone left, Seyyid sat with Qamar and his family and advised them to be patient and to recite Qur'an and give *sadaqa* for his father and do good deeds in his name.

After few weeks…

Sick Son

It was almost the time for *zuhr* prayers and one of the persons, Mr. Zahid who was a regular attendee of Seyyid's lectures came in a hurry and requested to talk to Seyyid urgently. Mr. Zahid told Seyyid that his son was very sick last week and had been hospitalized. He had a major surgery in emergency to save his life. At the time of admission in hospital, he only paid some of the required advance money as his financial condition was not good. On the third day, the hospital asked him to pay a huge sum so that they can do major surgery and take care of his son after it. Mr. Zahid said that he borrowed money from his boss and requested him to reimburse fixed amount from his monthly salary. In hurry, he took the money from his boss and went to the hospital. However, when Mr. Zahid went to the hospital accountant office to give the required money, the accountant checked in the computer and informed him that his brother had come the night before and deposited not only money for surgery but also a large extra amount sufficient for his son's stay in the hospital after surgery until his discharge. 'The hospital will return any remaining extra amount back to you', said the accountant. Mr. Zahid was shocked and told the accountant that he had no brother. However, the accountant said that the person introduced himself as his brother. Mr. Zahid asked if that person left his name, phone or any other contact details. The reply was negative as that person gave money in cash and left no details. Finally, Mr. Zahid asked about physical features and the accountant was upset and said that he deals with hundreds of hospital patients and their family members and doesn't remember him. Mr. Zahid came out of hospital, puzzled as to how to find that person….

Seyyid smiled and told Mr. Zahid that he should first thank God for this timely help and offer two *rak'at* prayer of thanks to God. Secondly, he should pray another two *rak'at* prayer for the person who helped him and also give *sadaqa* for him. 'You should always pray for that person after your prayers and in your night prayers as he has saved your dearest and most valuable asset of your life,' said Seyyid. It was time for *zuhr* by then so they performed their prayers with few others who had come to Seyyid's house.

After prayers, Mr. Zahid told Seyyid that among his family members there was no one who could pay the high amount of money for his son's surgery. He also mentioned that his own brothers and first cousins are not living in the city and they were not informed of his son's condition and so it is impossible that they may have paid. He also called other family members who could have paid the money and found that they were not informed of this son's condition and declined that they have paid… Mr. Zahid then said that the only place he could think of was Seyyid's house where they meet with several friends twice or thrice a week to pray and attend his lecture and so he thought someone from here may have done it. However, he didn't recall informing anyone in the gathering here when he came last time while his son was admitted in hospital. 'I left in hurry after *zuhr* prayers when my wife called from hospital to bring few medicines. Seyyid, please help me to find the person who has done this noble deed and saved the life of my son while remaining secret himself', he said. Seyyid smiled and said that he will help, but that Mr. Zahid should wait for a few days until his son recovers after surgery and is discharged from the hospital. He also said that he should come this Saturday and he will try to see what can be done.

Mr. Zahid's son was still in the hospital and was recovering fast and Mr. Zahid and his wife were happy and at the same time, trying to find out who the mysterious helper was. That afternoon, he received a phone call from Ahmad, a student very close to Seyyid, who asked him for urgent help with money. The amount was very small. He said that the money will be returned in a week's time. He said 'Dear brother Zahid, you are under no obligation to help me. I will ask another person to help me and it will not affect our relationship in the least.' Mr. Zahid, who was quietly listening to Ahmad, informed him that his son was in the hospital and had major surgery. Ahmad was surprised to hear this news and apologized to him and said that since he was having exams, he didn't come to Seyyid's house last week. However, Mr. Zahid said that he will be happy to give him the money on the condition that he will not inform Seyyid or anyone about it. Ahmad refused to take it. However, due to repeated and heavy insistence of Mr. Zahid, he was forced to take it. Ahmad provided details of his bank account number and Mr. Zahid immediately transferred the required amount. After a week, as per his promise, he returned the money to Mr. Zahid.

The next Saturday, after *maghrib* prayers, Seyyid gave a lecture on the characteristics of believers and their lifestyle. A lot of people were present, including the 12 students. He mentioned few basic things about the believers' intention and thinking, their life, their actions, their manners, their aim of life, their ways of dealing with different situations, their basic routines and their quest for hereafter. 'A true believer is a totally different human being. Though he may appear to be a common person, but he is very high in his status. He lives like a passenger in this world. He sees things, actions, events, and everything that happens around him with the eye of reality, with the divine vision blessed to him by God according to the level of his faith and knowledge. He is a very intelligent person though he may appear to be slow. He is not fooled by the crafty ways of this world. He doesn't go after his name, fame and transient glittering worldly returns', Seyyid continued... Everyone was immersed in the inspiring words of Seyyid. After the lecture, Seyyid announced that everyone should pray for the recovery of Mr. Zahid's son. He then said that someone has done a great deed by helping him and said that Mr. Zahid wants to know who that person is and thank him. However, no one from the audience responded. Seyyid then requested that if that person doesn't want to show himself in front of everyone, he should come to him in private and he will keep his secret. Everyone recited *salawat*.

After the dinner was over, Mr. Zahid stayed with Seyyid until everybody left. However, no one came to him or Seyyid. Mr. Zahid then thanked Seyyid for his help. Seyyid said that after your son is back to normal life, bring him here and then he will help to find out that person. Mr. Zahid then left thanking him.

Families of several friends and acquaintances who used to come to Seyyid's house visited his son in the hospital during the next few days. However, he and his wife couldn't get any information about the person who had helped. His wife asked from ladies of the families, but nobody was aware of anything about it. Mr. Zahid informed Seyyid about it. Seyyid smiled and said that the person who has helped his son must be of a very high IQ and cautious in protecting his deed. But he said that he will try to find out in a few days after he brings his son to Seyyid's house.

After four weeks, Mr. Zahid came to Seyyid's house with his son, Javad. It was before *maghrib* prayers. Some students were making preparations for the gathering of joy and happiness as it was the occasion of *wiladat* of Imam Ali (as). Seyyid kissed his son who was a boy of 13 years of age studying in 7th grade. Seyyid asked him about his health and studies. Then Seyyid asked Mr. Zahid that he should observe a few things today. When he will announce that today Mr. Zahid's son is here who has now fully recovered and recite *salawat* for his health, watch the faces of those who are near him, especially those 12 students. 'If someone smiles more than others, or shows a specific affectionate expression while looking at your son then surely that person has paid for his son's surgery. If this doesn't happen then watch who talks more to your son, makes him sit near him, shows more tender affection towards your son while you are here after prayers, during dinner and after it. If someone, especially one of those 12 students shows more affection or frequently smiles looking at your son's face, that person might have helped. You should then inform me and then I will ask that person in private,' said Seyyid. Mr. Zahid said that he will be vigilant and try to observe what he asked him.

After prayers, when Seyyid sat on his seat to give a lecture, he changed the routine and first asked Javad to come near him. Then he introduced Javad, told about his illness and said that some unknown person has helped and may God bless him. He then said prayers for Javad's health and requested everyone to recite *salawat*. He then began his lecture on fruits of patience in one's life. He said: 'Patience is the basic ingredient of faith. A patient person is a very powerful person because God is with him. However, most of the times in our daily lives, patience is forgotten and the person who has suffered a hardship or loss gets stressed. Patience keeps a person stable under the most difficult situations in life. It acts like a powerful shield. A successful person is always patient because he gets back what he lost, he achieves success, gets what he struggled for because patience is a divine mechanism that overrules all the events and material phenomena and guarantees one's success,' Seyyid said. He then described different levels of patience and their fruits and the skills necessary to develop patience.

'Finally when a person reaches the highest point of patience, he achieves the station of *rida*, or satisfaction with God in all circumstances. Beyond that there are other stations until God is satisfied with his servant, which is the last station', Seyyid concluded. Everyone was deeply in thought and paid utmost attention to the inspiring words of Seyyid. Mr. Zahid was carefully watching the faces of those 12 students and some others in the audience who were rich. However, he failed to detect any sign. They were all sitting and listening to Seyyid. No one showed any emotions on their faces. He looked at

Ahmad's face who was also smiling and saying *salawat* with others but dismissed the possibility of help from him since during those days Ahmad was himself in need of money and had asked him for help.

After the lecture, during dinner, people talked with Mr. Zahid and asked about his son, they also talked casually with Javad, asked about his health, studies etc. However, no one showed any special affection towards his son. Mr. Zahid took the hand of Ahmad and pulled him away from everyone and asked him about his exams. Ahmad said that the exams went very well and he thanked Mr. Zahid for his timely help with money. Mr. Zahid insisted that if he needed money, he should consider him as his real brother and ask him without any hesitation. Ahmad thanked him and promised that he will do the same.

When everyone left, Mr. Zahid told Seyyid that despite his close, keen and continuous observation, he couldn't detect anyone who showed specific affection towards his son as all were same in their good behavior. Seyyid said that he saw Ahmad was talking to his son, perhaps he may have helped. Mr. Zahid said that Ahmad himself was in need of some money during those days and so it is not possible. Seyyid asked Mr. Zahid how he knew this. Mr. Zahid said that Ahmad had called him for help about four days after the surgery of his son and that he was not aware of his son's sickness. Seyyid smiled. He then said that the person who helped him for his son's surgery was perhaps in the gathering today but was too smart to disclose himself. 'Perhaps we may never find him,' he said. However, he said that after a few weeks, he will try again. Mr. Zahid then thanked Seyyid and left with his son.

Difficult Lessons

Mr. Kumayl was sitting with his son and talking to Seyyid. He had come after several days and it was near *maghrib* prayers. Few other students were also there. 'Seyyid you know how busy life is. My son had appendix surgery few weeks ago and his exams are approaching. As you know, he is in 12th grade and must work hard so that he can enter a good university. Because of his surgery and the rest advised by the doctors, he has lagged behind a bit in his studies. Although he is very intelligent, I am still worried about Abbas's future,' he said. Seyyid smiled and looked towards Abbas and said: 'No don't worry. Abbas is very intelligent and smart and I am sure he will study hard and recover his loss in a short time and will do his best in exams.' Mr. Kumayl was still worried and requested Seyyid to pray for him. It was now time for *maghrib* prayers and everyone began doing *wuzu*. Most of Seyyid's students had arrived by then.

After *maghrib* prayers, Seyyid started his lecture. The topic was very interesting for the audience as Seyyid was talking on 'self-admiration' or *ujb*. He said that it is a dangerous disease and affects mostly those who are talented, such as top students, intellectuals and scholars, people with extraordinary skills and those who are in power and authority. 'If a person uses 'I' very often in his conversation, feels that he is 'something', loves his opinions, thinks that he never makes a mistake, and has difficulty in accepting his mistakes, he is possibly suffering from this disease. He may offer different explanations to defend himself that he is normal but in fact he is sick as he only sees himself. He is more likely to make errors and makes more enemies because he is blinded to previous mistakes, blames others and makes more mistakes in the future and every time, he covers them with his high IQ and superficial knowledge. An intelligent and realistic person is different. He has self-insight and sees himself with the eye of truth and attributes his successes and right opinions to the knowledge he has been bestowed by God and opportunities and helpers he has got. He takes his mistakes seriously, corrects them and doesn't feel ashamed to accept them. He is thus a good team worker, while a person with *ujb* can never be a good team worker as his social cognition is very limited and he fails to appreciate others as he thinks that he is always right.' Seyyid continued with his lecture and he then explained in detail the treatment and preventive strategies of this deadly disease. His lecture inspired everyone and awakened many of them, especially the university students who were particularly impressed and affected by his words. After lecture, most of them were quiet and pondering over themselves. After dinner, people left slowly, saying goodbye to each other.

Abbas woke up at *fajr*. He had slept late in night as he was studying. After prayers, he was checking his emails and found an interesting email title:

'Get top position in your high school exams – Try our unique email-based teaching program.'

He was curious and so opened the mail and found a deal for email-based learning program that was free for a week. It was from an online teacher who claimed to prepare students for grade 12 exams and guaranteed that if they follow the guidelines, they will score 80% or higher in their exams. However, the condition was that they should write their problems on daily basis and the teacher would reply next day with solutions and explanations. The teacher would take a test and ask questions randomly from the books. Abbas found it interesting and thought that since it is free for a week, he will benefit freely and then leave it. He then wrote two questions that were difficult for him each from physics, mathematics, chemistry and biology. Since he also had problems with certain basic concepts, he asked solutions to them also and sent the mail.

Abbas was curious as to when the reply will come and so after every few hours he was checking his email. He was on a study leave from his school and so he was usually in a public library near his house for his studies. After *maghrib* prayers, he went home and resumed studying. He slept at 11 in the night after checking mail and found that no answer had come from that online teacher. Next morning after *fajr*, when he checked his email, he was shocked with happiness. That online teacher had provided very clear answers to all his questions with figures from not only his grade 12 curriculum but also other books and had also attached few valuable tips for understanding the concepts he had difficulty in and had asked him. At the end of email, it said:

Ask me more – Your online teacher.

After Abbas downloaded and copied the answers to his computer, he thought for a while that the person must have spent at least 3 hours to write the answers for him. He then thought the fees he will charge after one week will be very expensive and so he immediately wrote email, thanking the online teacher for his nice and elaborate replies and giving his valuable time. He then asked 10 more questions and problems that were very difficult for him while going through the books yesterday and sent them. He thought that within next six days, he will try to 'use' this online teacher free of charge and solve all his major problems and leave him. Next day again after *fajr* prayers he checked his email and found that, as before, the replies sent by the teacher were very easy to understand. The answers were with extra figures and tables from other books and suggestions to write the answers to get maximum scores in exams. As usual the email ended with:

'Ask me more, dear student – Your online teacher.'

Within an hour Abbas first thanked the online teacher for his time and effort and again sent his new questions and problems he found yesterday. Abbas told his mother of this new online teacher scheme and said: 'Mother, I will get all my questions answered by this great online free teacher and then I will say thanks before leaving him at the end of one week.' His mother said that he should not do that. At least he should pay him some amount even though he hasn't asked for the 7 days free help he has provided to him. 'I will give you the money. You know that someone who teaches you actually makes you his subordinate. Imparting knowledge has no cost or returns. It's a highly valuable deed. At least you should show some respect to that teacher. You don't know why that person is spending valuable time to send you the answers. Perhaps that person has a sick member in his family and is hoping that you will pay money. And if tomorrow you get a good position in your exam, you will always feel guilty that you didn't pay the person,' she said. Abbas thanked his mother and agreed.

Days passed. Every day Abbas was reading his books and updating his knowledge and understanding based on the replies provided by the online teacher. Interestingly, this online teacher was creative in his approach and so Abbas learned several new ways to understand and reply the questions and solve the problems. On 7th day, when Abbas opened his mail, he got the answers as usual. Still about 30% work was remaining and so he estimated that if online teacher helped him, it will take about two more weeks. His exams were after three weeks. He decided to write in detail to the online teacher:

Dear online teacher
Salaam

God bless you. Many many thanks for your valuable time and guidance you have offered free of charge for the last seven days. Your answers and explanations and novel approaches have changed my basic understanding of all the subjects I have been studying since the last two years. I guess that you are a highly qualified knowledgeable person, perhaps a university professor.

I have utmost respect for you. May I ask you who you are and so I want to meet you personally and learn from you. Please send me your phone and address.

I want to pay you for the 7 days valuable teaching you provided to me. This is my mother's order to me and I must pay though you have offered it free. Kindly send your bank account number and the amount I have to pay. In addition, I wish to learn from you for two more weeks as my exams will start after three weeks and I wish to cover the whole curriculum with your new approach. Kindly, also let me know the amount for that too and I will pay in advance.

Many thanks and sincere prayers
Respectfully
Abbas

He then sent his questions in a separate email.

Within three hours Abbas got a reply from the online teacher. It read:

Dear Abbas
Salaam
Thanks for your email. May God bless you with more knowledge. I also wish to meet you; however, I have a busy schedule. I will inform you about the payments after two weeks when you finish your studies with me. I will also try to meet you then. Please pay attention to your studies. Please say my *Salams* to your respected mother and ask her to pray for me.

Thanks and du'a
Online teacher

Abbas was shocked to read the email. He was impressed by the trust that online teacher had put in him and his concern for him. He felt like this person is someone who knows him. It sounded like a bit unprofessional. However, due to pressure of exams, he dismissed the idea and started reading his course books again. At dinner, he told his family members about this online teacher's new email. Everyone was surprised. His father said that perhaps he is a student like you and so he asked your mother to pray for him. 'I am sure he is a young intelligent university student who is making his living by teaching online via email,' said Mr. Kumayl. 'Otherwise, these professional teaching centers charge a lot of money in advance and their quality is not good,' he continued. 'May God bless him with success in all his life endeavors,' Abbas's mother prayed for him. 'We will pay him whatever he asks,' Mr. Kumayl said. 'Abbas dear, you should take a break tomorrow and go to Seyyid's lecture at *maghrib*,' his mother suggested. Abbas agreed.

Next day, Abbas went to Seyyid's house before *maghrib*. Seyyid welcomed him and asked him about his studies and exams. Abbas told him about the online teacher and his great help. 'Seyyid, this teacher is exceptional. He has not charged me anything and he really cares for me. He compassionately wishes success for me and his style of answering questions and solving problems is really impressive. He gives me more than I ask him – every time,' Abbas said. Seyyid smiled and prayed for both of them. 'You are the seeker of knowledge and he is your teacher,' he said. 'But Seyyid, I feel like he knows me. He cares for me more than a professional online teacher does,' Abbas said and then looked at Seyyid's face for his response. Seyyid smiled and said: 'Maybe. But you should pay attention to your studies now and then pay him well after your learning is over with him. You should pray for him too.' Abbas agreed and thanked Seyyid.

After *maghrib* prayers, Seyyid gave an inspiring lecture on sincerity or *ikhlas*. He first recited *ayahs* of Qur'an and then mentioned few traditions on sincerity. Then he described the definition of a sincere action and the value of such an action in one's life and its impact in this world and the hereafter. He then explained in detail a hadith from Imam al-Sadiq (as): 'To persevere an action until it becomes sincere is more difficult than performing the action itself, and the sincerity of action lies in this that you should not desire anyone to praise you for it except God Almighty, and intention supersedes action. Lo, verily, intention is action itself...'

Seyyid then said that all our actions, including studying at university, professional work to earn living for family, meeting with friends and relatives and helping them, loving one's children, and all other actions, if they are done only with sincere intention to please God or as a duty towards Him, then they become accepted for divine reward. Most of the times these actions are rewarded in this world because they were done for minor returns and 'socialization' and directly or indirectly to please creatures.

Seyyid's lecture was an eye opener for many of those sitting there and he ended his lecture with the following sentence: 'One should remind himself of his duties and judge his intention and actions in the light of the verse of the Holy Qur'an:

قُلْ إِنَّ صَلَاتِي وَنُسُكِي وَمَحْيَايَ وَمَمَاتِي لِلَّهِ رَبِّ الْعَالَمِينَ

Say: "Truly my prayer and my service of sacrifice, my life and my death are (all) for Allah, the Lord of the Worlds. (6:162).

After the lecture, dinner was served and Abbas talked with a few of Seyyid's students. Most of them asked him about his studies and exams. He then left for home.

Days passed quickly and on the last day of the two weeks when his online teaching was over, Abbas requested the online teacher to send his bank account details and his name and address so that he can meet him. However, he didn't receive any reply. Abbas informed his mother and she said that is the online teacher may be sick. 'You should pray for him and pay attention to your own studies. Right now this is the most important thing for you,' she said. Abbas was very busy and stressed as exams were approaching. He didn't go out of his house and only studied. During his exams, he used all the creative approaches taught by the online teacher to answer the questions and solve the problems. He always remembered the unknown teacher and prayed for him. Finally, his exams finished after two weeks and then, the first thing he did was to write again to that online teacher to send his name and address. He wrote:

Dear respected teacher
Salam

God bless you. By the grace of God my exams went very well. I answered the questions according to the techniques and approaches taught by you. You have opened my mind to learn any new subject with different approaches. The three weeks of your teaching will have impact on my career in future. Thank you again.

Kindly send me your name, address, phone number so that I can meet you. Also send me your bank account number so that my father will send you the amount he has in his mind because he thinks that your impressive teaching deserves much more amount than what you perhaps have in your mind.

God bless you and eagerly waiting to meet you.

Respectfully yours
Abbas

After sending the email, Abbas was sure that his unknown teacher will reply. However, no reply came. He went to Seyyid and informed him about it. Seyyid smiled as usual and said to him that the online teacher is a very intelligent person and he will never want that you see him and give him money. 'He is a pious person who has done this good act for the sake of God,' said Seyyid. 'But Seyyid, he should realize that I can learn more from him if I meet him. By keeping himself unknown, he is indirectly denying me from learning from him,' said Abbas. Seyyid said that perhaps there are other reasons that he doesn't know. 'You should have good opinion of such a great man,' Seyyid said. Abbas realized his mistake and apologized to Seyyid. Then Seyyid said: 'You should give *sadaqa* for him and pray for him. Perhaps one day he will meet you if he thinks it is necessary.' Abbas agreed.

After three weeks, Abbas's result was announced. His name was among the top three students of the city and this meant that he was eligible for a government-funded scholarship to study abroad in any field he was interested in. He thanked his mother and father, they prayed for him and started informing relatives. Abbas's father called Seyyid and thanked him for his prayers and said that on Saturday he wishes to give dinner to all those who will come to his lecture. Abbas first went to Seyyid with sweets and kissed his hands. He remembered the unknown teacher and prayed for him. He told Seyyid, 'I wish he was here and I could meet him and learn more from him,' he said. Seyyid smiled and exhorted him to be patient and asked him to come on Saturday and inform his friends also. He said that he will announce that his father is giving special dinner for his success. 'This is to thank God for your great success in exam. If you go abroad on scholarship, you have to come back Abbas,' he said. Abbas thanked him and left for home.

After lunch, he wrote an email to the unknown teacher and informed him of his success. He then wrote:

Dear and respected teacher
Salaam

Kindly allow me to meet you and learn from you. I feel that by not meeting me you are denying imparting me knowledge and preventing me from learning more.

Please respond to this email as soon as possible.

Yours respectfully
Abbas

Next day, after *maghrib* he got a reply. That unknown teacher explained his denial of meeting with him as:

Dear Abbas
Salaam

I am very happy that you secured top position in your exams. I thank God for this opportunity. I know that you are eagerly wishing to meet me. However, I don't want to show myself to you because I have done this teaching as my duty and so I don't want any thanks or rewards for it.

However, because you have insisted so much, I will come to Seyyid's house on Saturday. But I will not introduce myself to you. You will see me but you will not know me as your teacher. Just bring sweets for everyone.

Du'a
Your unknown teacher

Abbas was stunned to read the email. He took a print and then went to his mother and showed her. He also told his father. They were all excited and impressed by this great person. 'I am sure he is a student of mathematics or computers or similar subject at university,' said his father. 'But father there are so many who are from universities who come to Seyyid's house,' replied Abbas. 'We will not know who this person is,' said his mother. '*Insha'Allah* we will know him,' said his father, Mr. Kumayl.

*****

'Brother Asad, sweets are not enough, you should take us to dinner at a restaurant. Your assignment was a great success and so it deserves more,' said Asad's younger sister. 'Okay I will,' replied Asad. His mother entered the room and found all her kids enjoying sweets. 'What is going on here?' she asked. 'Mother, remember few weeks ago I had an important assignment for my career promotion. Today the result was announced; I got third position in university. *Alhamdolillah*, now I can easily pass my other exams and write a great PhD thesis proposal,' replied Asad. His mother recalled few weeks ago Asad was sick but he was working almost 18 hours a day for three weeks to prepare for his assignment and she was worried about his health. '*Alhamdolillah*, great achievement my son. You have done nice job. God bless you with more successes in future,' his mother prayed for him. 'So now brother, where is our dinner?' They all were demanding from Asad, who was the eldest son. Finally, Asad agreed to take them to dinner that night.

*****

Next day, Abbas went to Seyyid and showed him the printed email. Seyyid smiled and said: 'Thank God. This person comes here and I am sure he is very smart to hide himself. I am sure we will never find him.' Abbas said that he will try to find him out. Seyyid just smiled.

On Saturday, Abbas came with his family much earlier to see everyone who comes and to find out his unknown teacher. His father was also with him in their search. But they couldn't find anyone's behavior 'abnormal'. Soon *maghrib* prayers started and after prayers, Seyyid gave a lecture on thanking God or *shukr*. He explained various characteristics of *shukr* and those who practice it. 'Thanking God doesn't mean that one should do *shukr* by tongue. It essentially means that one must realize by heart that all the blessings a person has are from God. One of the other prerequisites of thanking God is thanking the person who has done good, as without thanking the creature who deserves to be thanked, thanking God doesn't mean anything,' he continued. At the end, Seyyid introduced Abbas and talked about his brilliant success in exams and prayed for him. He said that the dinner and sweets tonight are from Mr. Kumayl. Then he also praised the unknown teacher who had helped Abbas to secure this great success. He thanked that teacher and said: 'God will reward you. As you have said, you are here but no one will recognize you, I believe in you that you did this great deed of imparting knowledge for the sake of God's pleasure and so you wish to hide yourself to avoid *riya'* and any reward. I thank you and so does Mr. Kumayl's family. Please recite *salawat* for the teacher.' While Seyyid was talking, Abbas was looking at a few faces that he thought were studying mathematics, computer sciences or similar subjects at universities, to detect if any one of them smiled or showed strong expression, perhaps that person might be his teacher. But he couldn't detect anything. They were all the same. His father too was looking around at faces of young people in the gathering, but he too couldn't detect anything.

While dinner was being served from Abbas's family, everyone was helping out, which was a routine at Seyyid's house. At the end of dinner, Abbas personally took the sweets and offered to everyone himself. He did this to see the guests from near and if someone showed an emotional expression or talked 'extra', that person would be his teacher. However, he failed again as everyone thanked him. Many people gave him gifts and prayed for him. Finally, everyone left one by one and in the end, Mr. Kumayl's family was left with Seyyid. They all thanked Seyyid and his efforts. Mr. Kumayl said: 'Respected Seyyid. This was your great ethical training to do pure action sincerely for the sake of God and so this pious teacher has remained unknown as he only wished his reward from Him.'

Seyyid just smiled and prayed for all of them and especially for Abbas. 'Abbas you have to be like this unknown teacher in the future,' he said. Abbas quickly replied: 'Sure I will be, *Insha'Allah.*'

In the afternoon of the next day, Seyyid saw an envelope pasted at his gate. Seyyid opened it and found a typed note in it:

Esteemed Seyyid
Salam
Thanks for teaching us to do '*birr*'. Job done only with *toufiq* of God. Please pray so that I keep it with me until I die.
Your humble student

Seyyid smiled and pondered deeply for a few minutes…he thanked God and prayed for the person.

Surprise Donation

Ibrahim's mother was worried about her son's unexpected picnic trip. She was not happy as there was an emergency in their family. 'How long will it take son? When will you return?' asked his mother. 'You know that Salim is in hospital, his kidneys have failed. They are our first degree relatives, he is your uncle's son and you should be with Salim, he is your first cousin. Remember what Seyyid said a few days ago in his lecture about keeping good relations with your near relatives. I will complain to Seyyid about your irresponsible behavior,' his mother continued. Ibrahim replied that he was only going for four weeks and he will keep in touch with Salim on phone. 'Mother, you know these are summer holidays after my annual exams and this is the only time I have to enjoy and take some rest,' he continued. He then promised his mother that he will call Salim daily. He tried very hard to convince her and make his mother happy until she finally gave him permission.

Ibrahim's father was supportive of his trip and he dropped him to the airport. He knew that his son is a grown up person and that his university education is tough enough to make him exhausted after exams. They were a rich family and had very close relations with his brother, Salim's father. Unfortunately, few days back, Salim got sick and was admitted to hospital. His medical tests showed that both of his kidneys had failed to function. Day before yesterday, the doctors recommended transplantation of healthy kidney from a matched donor in the family. While saying goodbye at the airport, Ibrahim's father asked him to call Salim and his parents as they were close family relatives and they had always helped them. Ibrahim promised to do so. He then said to his father that Seyyid loved him very much and he was close to him and he didn't want

Seyyid to be unhappy with him. ‘Pappa, as mother may complain to Seyyid about my trip at this time, I request you to tell Seyyid that after exams, I needed rest and this is important for my health too. Seyyid has also told us in his lectures that God loves those who take care of themselves in all aspects of their lives and will ask about how one took care of his body and health in this world.’ His father promised to tell Seyyid about it. Ibrahim left for his picnic trip….

Dr. Sajjadi, famous kidney transplantation surgeon, said that they cannot perform kidney donation match tests on two brothers of Salim as they were too young for it. Salim’s father had heart disease and so he too was not a candidate. Salim’s mother had diabetes. The family was in real trouble. Ibrahim’s father and mother went and gave their blood for possible kidney donation. Ibrahim’s sister was married and since she had a young son, she was not a suitable candidate. Ibrahim’s own brother was too young and Dr. Sajjadi, despite much insistence from his father refused to take sample. They were looking for donation from other family members.

Ibrahim’s father went to see Seyyid and explained the situation of Salim and his family. He requested Seyyid to pray and announce at the Saturday gathering if anyone wishes to donate kidney. He said whatever amount the person wants, he will pay for it. Seyyid promised to inform those who will attend the lecture on the coming Saturday. Ibrahim’s father also informed Seyyid about his son’s trip to the north of the country after exams. Seyyid smiled and said: ‘Don’t worry, I know Ibrahim very well.’

On Saturday evening after his lecture, Seyyid announced that Salim needed a kidney to save his life and if anyone wishes to donate, they can contact Ibrahim’s father. He asked them to recite a *salawat* for him and to pray for his health and recovery. Everyone present in Seyyid’s lecture was moved to hear this news and they wanted to help in whatever way possible. Seyyid provided the contact details of Ibrahim’s father after lecture.

Next day, about 30 individuals went to the hospital, met Ibrahim's father and then contacted Dr. Sajjadi's office. Most of them were young. These included 11 students who were close to Seyyid. They all had their medical checkup and general medical tests. After that, their samples for kidney match were taken. Dr. Sajjadi told Ibrahim's father that it will take about 7 days for the samples to be matched and get the final results. However, he said, the best match comes from the nearest family member and it guarantees long viability and less rejection of the donated kidney.

Ibrahim was calling Salim and his family every night and asking about his health. They informed him of the announcement made by Seyyid and that 30 persons gave their samples for donation of their kidney. Ibrahim's father asked him about the trip and he told that the mountains were beautiful in summer and he was enjoying his trip. His mother told him to shorten his trip and come back if he can. Ibrahim told her that he will try his best.

Five days later, Salim's father received a call from Dr. Sajjadi's office that he should come immediately. They have good news for him. When he reached hospital, he was informed that the hospital's branch in another big city that has sophisticated techniques for faster and more accurate matching for tissue samples have received an anonymous kidney donation for Salim. This sample is very close to the Salim's body tissue for donation acceptance. 'How much is the cost asked by the anonymous donor?' asked Salim's father. Dr. Sajjadi's secretary replied that the donation was free. 'This is common practice. Many people give free donations of their kidneys. The donated kidney will be here in the next few hours. We will only charge you the cost of transportation.' Upon hearing this news, both families became happy and thanked God as well as the anonymous donor. Salim's father went to Dr. Sajjadi's office again that evening and asked about the identity of the donor. He was told that this is not possible because this information is with the other branch of the hospital that had sent the kidney and they probably know. He took the contact number of the public relations office of the hospital in another city from where the donation had come. However, he was told that it was not possible as the donor wants to remain anonymous and has put a legal restriction. If the physician who operated upon the donor disclosed his name, the donor can legally sue him as well as the hospital in the court of law for the breach of confidentiality.

Ibrahim's mother was particularly happy that Salim's life will be saved. She called Ibrahim that night. 'My son, God has saved Salim's life. A servant of God has given a kidney donation. I wish you were here with us. He will be operated tomorrow evening, try to come back if you can.' Ibrahim replied: 'Thank God. Salim is saved. I will call him in a few minutes. Mother it is so beautiful here. I wish all of you were here with me now.' Ibrahim's mother instinctively asked why his voice appeared weak and frail. 'Are you normal?' she asked. He replied that he was normal. 'The weather is different here so that might have affected my throat,' replied Ibrahim. His mother thanked God that her son had no major problem. Salim's surgery was successful. He was back home within ten days after surgery and started a near normal life. Seyyid was informed about the whole story of anonymous donation and successful surgery by Ibrahim's father and he too was happy and informed everyone after his lecture of the good deed done by the anonymous donor. Everyone prayed for Salim's health.

Ibrahim returned from his successful and enjoyable picnic trip after one month. All the family members including his uncle and aunt went to the airport to welcome him. When they saw him, they were surprised that he appeared a bit slim. When asked about the reason, Ibrahim replied that he did a lot of mountain climbing during one month and ate natural food. 'I lost 8 kg,' said Ibrahim. '*Masha Allah* my son is healthier now,' said Ibrahim's mother. Ibrahim apologized to his uncle and aunt for his absence. They said that there was no need for it as they were aware of his difficult studies and hard work at the university and that he has a bright career ahead of him for which his must work hard. He immediately went to Salim's home and met him.

They both met as if they had been away for years. Salim was a bit unhappy with him that he didn't stay while he was undergoing difficult time with his kidney failure and surgery. 'You were enjoying the trip in north while I was having difficult time here,' said Salim. Ibrahim first apologized to him and asked Salim to forgive him. Then he said that it was necessary for him to take rest. 'You know how difficult my studies are. You are usually doing business with your father while I have to study hard to make my career.' 'You are right, brother. Both of us had a test from God,' said Salim. He was highly praising the great unknown donor and that he didn't charge any money for his donation. Ibrahim said may God bless him. Ibrahim then said that he will give a dinner at Seyyid's house after his Saturday lecture to compensate for his absence. Salim was overjoyed and thanked him. All the family members appreciated that Ibrahim kept his friendship and they all were very happy.

Next Saturday, all the family members were present at Seyyid's house and they attended *maghrib* prayers and then his lecture. Before lecture, Seyyid told everyone about the dinner that it was from Ibrahim to compensate for his absence during his cousin Salim's sickness and surgery. He then said that *silaye rahmi* (keeping good relations with near relatives) is a very important obligation for all Muslims. 'It makes one live longer and happier and increases one's sustenance,' he said. He then praised Salim for forgiving Ibrahim and Ibrahim for compensating his absence. Then all of them attended lecture on enjoining good and forbidding evil in a modern society. 'Without enjoining good and forbidding evil, a society can never be healthy. It is the most valuable and the most difficult task as it puts a person's prestige at stake and sometimes can take a person's life. One has to be very smart to enjoin good and forbid evil as there are several ways to do it and at every place, a different style has to be adopted depending upon the situation. A lot of people do not enjoin good and do not forbid evil things, practices, norms and actions in the society because they think this is not their duty. This is a serious error. Without it, the society slowly becomes corrupted until it becomes a normal culture of the society,' he said. Seyyid also talked about various modern techniques and tools to promote good and forbid evil. 'Every person has to enjoin good and forbid according to the level of status, education, respect and authority he has', he said. After his lecture, they had dinner. Seyyid was with the families of Salim and Ibrahim and he was closely watching Ibrahim.

After most of the family members and attendees had left, Seyyid called Ibrahim. 'How are you dear Ibrahim? You look a bit weaker. Was your health okay during the trip?' Ibrahim said that he was normal and that he did some exercise and ate a lot of natural food there. 'As you know Seyyid, when we, who live in the city here, go to a place at a higher altitude in the mountains, the weather and food are different and it affects our health too. In the beginning, I felt a bit weaker but then I did mountain climbing and enjoyed life. I thanked God for all the good things,' said Ibrahim. Seyyid asked him a direct question: 'Are you hiding anything from me?' Ibrahim smiled with a surprise and said: 'Seyyid, you are my dear and respected teacher. Why should I hide when God knows everything?' Seyyid smiled back at his intelligent reply and prayed for him.

They all left saying thanks and goodbye to Seyyid.

*****

Marriage Proposal

It had been several days that Husayn was thinking of talking to his mother about plans for his marriage. He was a final year medical student and very intelligent in his studies. He was planning to finish his MD and then go for specialization in surgery and wished that his wife be a doctor too. In his university, they had weekly sessions of *du'a* Kumayl and other religious gatherings where students interacted. He knew that Sobhan's sister was a junior medical student in his university. He had seen her at the *du'a* Kumayl sessions and had also exchanged a few words about work related to organizing events there. He was impressed by her modest behavior and good manners.

Sobhan's family was of very noble background and the training given by Sobhan's parents to their children was exceptional. All of their sons and daughters were very well-mannered, knowledgeable and their lifestyle was truly exemplary. Once or twice a year, Husayn and other friends from Seyyid's students attended gatherings at Sobhan's house. Husayn truly admired Sobhan's family. Husayn thought that today evening was a very appropriate time to talk to his mother for seeking the hand of Sobhan's sister. Sometimes Husayn felt a very strong admiration for her and prayed to God that she be his wife.

At *zuhr* time, Husayn went to Seyyid's house and without disclosing the name or identity of the person he was interested in, he asked Seyyid's opinion about how to go for a marriage proposal. Seyyid smiled and prayed for him. He said that you should re-evaluate the reason for your attraction or interest towards a particular person for marriage. What attracts you? Is it the physical characteristics? Is it wealth? Is it the social status? Or is it some godly or divine quality in her that you feel like marrying her will be good for you. He said 'You should first pray two *rak'at* prayers and ask God's favor for your marriage. Then as you have planned, you should talk to your mother and then father and seek their opinions too. They are more experienced and know you better.' Husayn thanked Seyyid and said that he will be in touch with him for further advice and left after *zuhr* prayers to his home. He told his mother that tonight, after *maghrib*, he wanted her help over an important issue. She replied by saying that it will be very good that he going to seek her advice.

It was around 3 pm and Husayn's mobile phone rang. It was Vaheed at the other end and he was in an urgent need to discuss a personal matter with Husayn and ask for his advice. He said that the matter was very important and affecting his personal life and that during the past few days, he was not able to focus on his studies. He wanted to see Husayn that same evening. Husayn asked Vaheed to come over to his house before *maghrib* prayers.

Vaheed was also a medical student and he and Husayn were classmates. They were good friends for the past several years. Vaheed also belonged to a good family and his father was a professor and all his uncles were highly educated, well settled in their lives. Vaheed's two brothers and sisters were in universities and among the top students of their classes. He and some of his family members were regular attendees of Saturday lectures of Seyyid. But Vaheed was closer to Seyyid than the rest of his family members. In fact, last week he went to meet Seyyid to seek his advice about this particular issue that was affecting his studies. He didn't mention exactly what the matter was as it was too early to seek his advice. Seyyid gave some supplications to recite and taught some psychological methods to reduce distraction and increase his focus on studies. Vaheed was feeling better but wanted to discuss the issue with Husayn and then go forth for the next step.

When Vaheed went to Husayn's house, he said salams to Husayn and also saw his mother. He said salams to her as well. His mother asked if all his family members were fine and ask Vaheed to convey her salams to them as well. Husayn took Vaheed to his room. His mother was curiously watching both of them. She said that she will send tea and snacks to his room.

Vaheed began talking about his problem…and Husayn was silent… shocked, but he controlled himself and continued to listen to Vaheed for almost 10 minutes without any expression or reaction on his face. Vaheed said that he was serious in getting married and he admired and was emotionally attracted to Sobhan's sister. She was the same person Husayn was planning to talk about to his mother that very evening after *maghrib* prayers. Vaheed finished his emotional conversation and sought Husayn's advice if this lady was appropriate for him or not. 'You are my best friend whom I can trust and I need your opinion. If you think she's suitable, I will ask my mother who might have some concerns because she has seen someone else for me, and convince her with your help. If you say no, then of course I will follow my mother's advice and go for her choice. That family is also as good as Sobhan's. Whatever you say brother,' he said.

Husayn, who was silent until that moment, asked Vaheed to wait and read Qur'an for a few minutes until he comes back with tea and snacks his mother had prepared.

Husayn went to another room and sat silent for a few moments and asked God's help to give him strength to control his emotions. He was puzzled and shocked. He then calmly thought that if he advises Vaheed to seek what his mother wishes for him, everything will be okay and he will also be able to talk to his own mother tonight for his own proposal with Sobhan's sister. No problem would occur then, no one's feelings would be hurt. For a while it seemed fair to him. But then…suddenly he recalled what Seyyid said few weeks ago about '*birr*'. Husayn now clearly understood that this was a test from God and that he should make the right but a tough decision now. After all, Vaheed was a believer and a very good person. For this very reason, he should respect Vaheed's personal choice over his own. So, after giving some thought, he asked God to help him control his emotions and make him stable. He then went to his mother, took the tea and snacks and entered his own room with a firm decision.

Vaheed was reading Qur'an when Husayn entered the room. He looked at Husayn. Husayn asked him how he was feeling. Vaheed said that he was waiting for his advice and help. 'Well my brother, I think Sobhan's sister is the best choice for you. If you allow me, let us talk to my mother because Sobhan's mother is a very close friend of hers and she also knows your mother. Your proposal is done. Let us see then how Sobhan's family responds,' said Husayn. Vaheed jumped in the air... 'Thanks brother,' he said and hugged Husayn. They then had their tea and snacks. It was *maghrib* time then. They performed their prayers together. Then, Husayn asked Vaheed to pray the two *rak'at* prayers Seyyid asked him to pray before taking practical steps for proposal. Then Husayn went out of the room to bring his mother.

'Sobhan's family is very good and suits you my son.' said Husayn's mother to Vaheed. 'But auntie, my mother has some other family in her priority. She knows that I am inclined towards Sobhan's sister very much. Can you please talk to her?' requested Vaheed. 'Why not, I will call her now. I will also call Sobhan's mother if your mother allows me,' said Husayn's mother. 'Thank you very much auntie.' Vaheed was quick to thank her.

Husayn's mother then called Vaheed's mother and informed her about Sobhan's family, their status and her son's inclinations to marry their daughter. She also said that Vaheed is like her own son, Husayn, and that she personally knows Sobhan's sister. Both the mothers discussed this important issue for a few minutes. Finally, Vaheed's mother was convinced and requested her to allow her to seek Vaheed's father's opinion.

Vaheed's mother then called back in a few minutes and said that Vaheed's father says Salams to her and has agreed. He has also requested that as she was a close friend of Sobhan's mother, she kindly talk to her about the proposal. Vaheed and Husayn were patiently watching how their mothers talked and how fast things were moving forward. Husayn's mother then called Sobhan's mother and as usual, both invited each other over and talked on different family issues. Finally, Husayn's mother said to her: 'Sister, I have another son that you probably also know. His name is Vaheed, the son of.....' She then praised Vaheed and his family. Sobhan's mother was an intelligent person and soon understood why her close friend brought Vaheed in the conversation today. She said: 'Sister, why don't you and Vaheed's mother come to our house next Friday and we will have a talk in everyone's presence. By that time, I will also discuss this matter with my husband and daughter. I would also like to take Seyyid's opinion if everything is okay. How about all of us going to his lecture on Saturday evening?' Both the mothers agreed.

Vaheed then thanked Husayn and promised a dinner if all went well and his proposal was accepted. He also planned to see Seyyid the next day and tell him what happened today so that he can get his support on Saturday. He then left. Husayn's mother came to his room and said: 'So son this was the problem you wanted to discuss with me today after *maghrib*? See how God helped!' Husayn replied 'Yes mother. Many many thanks. I pray all goes well and that we see Vaheed married to Sobhan's sister soon.' His mother said that she is now concerned about him too and will look for a good bride of his match too. Husayn smiled and said: 'Thank you dear mother.'

That night Husayn felt elevated, free and calm. He had never experienced such a state before in his life. It was difficult for him to sleep because of the inner joy he was experiencing. He then read Qur'an and read supplications. He woke up early before *fajr* and prayed his night prayers and thanked God for his favor and sought his help for keeping this important deed secret.

Next day, Vaheed went to see Seyyid at *zuhr* prayers. After prayers, he sat close to Seyyid and told him the reason why he came earlier last week and then about what had happened the day before at Husayn's house and how Husayn and his mother had helped the proposal for his marriage. Seyyid was surprised at first and then he smiled and said: '*MashaAllah* you have made the right choice and the right move. You should be very thankful to Husayn for it.' Vaheed said that he will give a dinner to Husayn after his marriage proposal goes well. Seyyid said: 'No, Husayn deserves much more. Do you know the *thawab* of introducing two parties to meet and making them agree upon marriage? It is equal to 70 Hajj! But he deserves still more.' Vaheed asked him the reason and he said that it is because Husayn has sincerely helped him for the sake of God. Then Seyyid gave him few general guidelines about marriage and how he should behave with his wife and her family members if all goes well.

Husayn visited Seyyid on Thursday morning and knew that Vaheed had visited him earlier. Seyyid welcomed him with a smile. He was then a bit curious and asked him: 'Dear Husayn, why did you come to me for marriage proposal earlier this week? I thought it was for your own marriage and that you liked someone. Isn't it?' Husayn looked at Seyyid's face with a smile and said: 'Dear teacher, you have taught us to do good deeds for our brother as if we are doing it for ourselves. Based on this, it didn't make any difference if this was for Vaheed or for myself,' Seyyid admired his reply and wanted to know more. 'So it was for Vaheed?' he asked. Husayn replied: 'He is my brother, so it was for him.' Seyyid smiled again at his answer and prayed for him. Husayn then said good bye to him and left for his university.

On Friday, both the families and Husayn's mother met. Overall, it was positive and Sobhan's family and his sister had no disagreements with Vaheed's family. It was then decided that next day they will all go to Seyyid's house before *maghrib* and attend his lecture and finally seek his opinion about dowry and other issues since he knew both the families very well and their kids were close to him.

After *maghrib* prayers on Saturday, Seyyid gave lecture on ideal family life and mutual duties of husband and wife in a modern society. He explained several delicate points that a couple should take care of while living in a sophisticated busy life of a modern city and how to take care of each other in a better way and train children according to the Islamic principles. Everybody appreciated his depth and pragmatic approach to solve minor problems that affect families especially newly married couples.

After the dinner was over and only two families and Husayn and his mother were left, Seyyid took them inside his living room. They were surprised to see the simplicity of Seyyid's family life. His wife welcomed them. They all sat on sofas and looked at Seyyid as he was the judge to pass a final judgment. Seyyid recited a few verses of Qur'an and Islamic traditions related to marriage and then looked at Vaheed and Sobhan's sister and smiled. He then asked Sobhan's father if he agreed with the marriage proposal. He replied: 'Seyyid we have agreed, but your approval is the final word. You know both the kids, in fact they are your kids not ours.' Vaheed's father said similar words. Seyyid then said a few words of advice on the simplicity of marriage and avoidance of unnecessary rituals as they bring *bala* (difficulties and hardships) for the newly married couples. He then said that if Sobhan's sister agrees, her *mehr* will be 5 gold coins. He then looked at her. She kept quiet and then said: 'I agree, Seyyid.' Every one recited *salawat*. Seyyid then proposed that after 10 days, it will be *wiladat* of Hazrat Fatima (sa) and that it will be a very auspicious day for their *nikah* at his house. They all agreed. Seyyid then thanked Husayn and his mother and said that it was their sincere effort for Vaheed that brought the two families closer to tie this heavenly knot for their son and daughter. He was having a deep look at Husayn. He kissed his forehead in front of everyone and prayed for him. Husayn's mother said to Seyyid: 'Seyyid, I request you to find a bride for him.' Seyyid smiled and said: '*InshaAllah*, I will.' They then thanked Seyyid and left together. Soon preparations for their marriage began and Husayn was forgotten.

Husayn thanked God that his secret had remained a secret as Seyyid was not able to find it and perhaps no one ever will…

Transport

'It's getting late Asad. You must prepare yourself to reach in time. Today you have an exam.' said Asad's mother. 'Your motorcycle is no doubt very good but winter is coming and it will take nearly an hour for you to reach university. Come on, get ready and take your breakfast.' Asad came out of his bed and said: 'Thanks mother. Today I will take the bus for university. Don't worry, I will reach in time.' And then Asad hurriedly prepared himself and left for university. It was a usual scene every morning. Some days, Asad would go by bus while at others he went riding on his motorbike.

Asad was a computer engineering student in one of the top universities. He was doing his PhD and had secured a scholarship because of his very good grades in entrance exams. He belonged to a middle class family and had two sisters and two brothers, all of whom were studying in colleges and universities. He was the eldest and had to struggle hard to make his career and prepare to support his family as his father was going to retire next year. He was very close to Seyyid and regular in attending his lectures every Saturday. Sometimes he would visit Seyyid's house to take his advice on personal and ideological issues. Asad's brothers and sisters also used to attend his lectures whenever they had time. Asad's parents had brought up their children in such a way that they always practiced self-respect and never complained about any deficiency and never aspired to high material comforts in their lives.

The exam was over and Asad was preparing to select courses for the next semester and also writing his research proposal for PhD research. While going downstairs from his department, he saw a notice pasted on the wall that read "**Top Computer Sciences PhD Students, Win Cash Awards and Prizes**". The notice provided few other details. Asad noted them and the email and phone number given at the end for contact. While on his way back home, he called the mobile number; however, no one replied. After few minutes, his mobile rang and it was a Telegram message. He was added to a new group "Top PhD Students Scholarships Forum". He found out that it was a new group with 10 members. There was an announcement which said that there is a golden opportunity for PhD students in computer sciences to win young scientist award. They have to send their CV, letter of recommendation from research supervisor and synopsis of their research proposal to an e-mail which was given in the message. They will have a choice between a cash award which was limited to 2000 dollars or that they let the scholarship award committee to choose the prize item which could possibly be much more. The deadline was three weeks and prizes were going to be announced within a week after that. Asad saved this announcement in his computer and noted the mobile number of the scholarship forum. He was curious as to who was the sponsor of this group and decided to call the next morning. But before that, he started working on his proposal and planned to finish it within a week.

Next morning, he called the number, however, no one picked and it was on message and so Asad left a message that he was interested in participation and that he wanted to know about the sponsor of this scholarship scheme. He then went to university library. Winter was near and so it was becoming difficult for him and his brothers and sisters to go to their institutions.

Within the next five days, Asad finished his proposal and gave it to his supervisor Prof. Hameed. His results were also announced and he had once again secured top position in all the courses he had taken that semester. Prof. Hameed was very happy with him. He informed Prof. Hameed about the scholarship forum and their conditions. Prof. Hameed agreed and gave him the letter of recommendation but was a bit concerned about sending the synopsis by email. He said to Asad to ask them if they can accept only the extended abstract. Asad called the number again and left the message.

After about three hours, he got a Telegram message from the same number that it was okay to send an extended abstract. Next day, Asad sent the CV, a letter from Prof. Hameed and the extended abstract of his research proposal by email.

*****

'Papa, I want to give back this new BMW you gave me.' said Yusuf. 'It doesn't suite me. Its seats are so soft that I feel like sleeping while driving. Besides, I feel a bit proud when I go to university and also to Seyyid's house.' His father was quietly listening to his only son's arguments against the expensive gift he had given him a few days ago over top class performance in his MBA exams. Yusuf was his only son and was being trained to take over his vast business after a few years. 'Okay my son, if you really think this car doesn't suit you, go ahead and give it back to Mr. Ameen's show room and get another one,' said his father. 'But Papa, I will keep the money in my account if I buy another car. Agreed?' His father smiled at his son and said: 'Agreed my son. But don't buy a more expensive car!' Yusuf agreed. It was near *maghrib* and so Yusuf decided to go to Seyyid's house.

It was Wednesday and Seyyid usually would give short interactive lectures that were of interest for young students who would come to meet him and requested him to talk. They would ask questions in the middle of the lecture. Today, there were some students and a few others. All of Seyyid's favorite ones were also present. After prayers, Seyyid started the lecture on the topic 'qualities of knowledgeable persons.' He began with an ayah of Qur'an:

...وَاتَّقُوا اللَّهَ وَيُعَلِّمُكُمُ اللَّهُ...

Be wary of Allah, and Allah shall teach you [2:282].

Seyyid explained how fearing God or keeping His thought in mind makes one knowledgeable. He said that it was because it leads to several basic changes in human thinking. A person who keeps God in mind will be a good observer of nature and ponder over it to see the wisdom behind everything created. Thus, he will develop the habit of becoming a deep thinker. He will also be more focused in his thinking and will make choice of the best because he takes this life as a test from God and to serve Him in the best manner and so he will also avoid distractions. As he remembers that one day he has to go back to God, this will also make him quick in performing his work. He will automatically develop patience over failures and setbacks during knowledge acquisition process because he knows that God is all-knower and will help him acquire more knowledge…. He explained several aspects of God fearing that have an impact on knowledge acquisition. Everyone was just amazed as to how Seyyid was fluently talking with soft composure as if he has gone through all these things he is saying.

After the lecture, Asad asked him a question: ‘Seyyid how it is possible for a knowledgeable person to be humble? What I usually see in my university is that students who are intelligent and even many faculty members are proud in their behavior only because they know something more than others.’ Seyyid smiled and said: ‘This is perhaps normal. It is because they are in the beginning stages of knowledge acquisition. When a person goes into the depth of knowledge and finds that there is a vast unending ocean in front of him that he doesn’t know, then he automatically realizes his own ignorance of so many things and he becomes humble. He becomes self-aware of his ignorance and the limits of his own knowledge. Another reason for being proud is that such persons have worldly aims for the acquisition of knowledge and so they behave proudly. A third reason is that they don’t realize that after every act of pride there will be a fall of humility for them. They will suffer a situation whereby they will be belittled. It is very interesting to see that there are over 30 characteristics of knowledgeable persons that are mentioned in Islamic traditions, and the first one is humbleness, then truthfulness, softness, compassion, good intention, visiting the learned, engaging in discussion with knowledgeable, loyalty and so on.' Then they all started talking informally with Seyyid. Asad informed him about his next semester preparations.

As they wanted to leave, Seyyid said that they should wait as he will bring some sweets because Asad had secured top position in his exams. Everyone recited *salawat.* They all had sweets together. Seyyid prayed for Asad's success and also for all of them. One by one, all of them congratulated Asad. Yusuf was sitting away and didn't talk much with Asad like others and he left earlier. Seyyid was closely watching his behavior but said nothing. They all then left saying goodbye to each other and to Seyyid.

Next day, Yusuf went to Mr. Ameen's show room and told him that he didn't like the car and wanted to have another one. Mr. Ameen welcomed the rich guest, as Yusuf's family members and relatives were his regular customers. He asked Yusuf which car he wanted. Yusuf asked him to show new models of Korean cars and Mr. Ameen was a bit surprised at his choice. Ameen said that he was tired of these expensive cars and wanted to have a 'change'. He said: 'Mr. Ameen, you know me very well. If I didn't like it, I will come again to you and then get a better one. I only have to talk to my father.' Mr. Ameen smiled and then showed him some new cars and finally Yusuf selected one. Mr. Ameen told him that the cost of the new one he had chosen was nearly one third of the BMW model he had. Yusuf then asked him to do the paper work for buying and transfer the balance to his personal account number. Mr. Ameen said that within two days this will be done.

Within two days, Yusuf had his new car and the remaining money was in his bank account. His father was surprised and his mother was not happy that her son was becoming spoiled. 'Mother, let me have a variety. This car is new, but it's a bit different from the previous one.' He defended himself. 'But you are changing things as if this has become your habit and this is not good. God doesn't like extravagant persons,' said his mother. 'But dear mother, this time I have got a cheaper car,' He replied. However, his mother said that she will see for how many days he will keep it. Yusuf promised that he will not buy a new car next time without her permission and made her happy. His father said that Yusuf is surely going to buy another one within the next three weeks. 'I know my son,' he said. His mother replied: 'Okay let us see who wins. He has promised me. I am sure he will keep it.'

*****

Three weeks later, Asad got a surprise email of congratulations that he has won the scholarship award. They also asked his bank account and other details. He was asked to reply and inform them of his choice whether he wanted 2000 dollars or allow the scholarship sponsors to choose gift for him. They also informed his supervisor Prof. Hameed who gave him a congratulations call and asked him to take the award. Everyone was happy. Such occasions were not uncommon in Asad's family, as all of them used to win such prizes. However, this was a big amount, not won by anyone before. At dinner, his brothers and sisters were giving their opinions on the two choices. Seeing their enthusiasm, Asad decided to take a vote. Four votes out of seven were in favor of giving sponsors the choice. Asad immediately replied to the email by saying that he gives the choice to the sponsors.

*****

'Mother, I really like my new car. It's really good. I feel very comfortable driving it. Why don't you allow me and Maryam to go for a week-long trip to my auntie's house? Hasan and Ameer want to learn a few basics of their sociology and business ethics courses from me and Fatima also wants to spend time with Maryam and learn mathematics. It's just a three hour drive, 200 km is not far.' said Yusuf. 'Ask your father,' replied his mother. Yusuf and his sister Maryam were waiting for their father to come back home in the evening. At dinner, Yusuf took the opportunity to request his father to allow them to go. He also winked at his sister to make her request. Yusuf's father knew that they both loved their aunt's kids and so he agreed on one condition. 'Both of you will take your books with you and study there. I know you are very responsible but I want to make sure that you will study,' he emphasized. 'We promise, Papa,' they both said. 'Thank you very much. If you allow us, we will leave tomorrow morning,' they said. Their parents agreed, but their mother was a bit concerned. However, Yusuf convinced her that he will drive carefully. They left the next morning.

*****

After three days, Asad was informed by email that he has won a new car. The address of the show room was provided and he was told that all the paperwork had been already done. He only had to go and submit a valid copy of his national ID and see the car model and choose the color of the car and get the ownership documents already prepared for him. He was asked to call someone by the name of Mr. Qadir. Asad was reading the email and thinking that he was in a dream. He thanked God and then informed his mother, father and everyone at home. They were all happy. All his brothers and sisters asked him to give them a dinner. Asad promised. They all planned to go to the showroom together the next morning. But Asad's father was a bit concerned. He asked Asad to immediately write an email of thanks and then ask who the sponsors were. He should get their address and go to see them personally and make sure that they were not involved in any illegal business or activity as they might use Asad in future. Asad told his father that they had called Prof. Hameed and so he probably knows them. But he wrote the email accordingly to please his father. No reply came until next morning. He then left a Telegram message. Reply came immediately that he should get the prize car and Mr. Qadir will inform him about the address etc. Asad then told his father that first, he will go to see Seyyid and seek his opinion and then if he agrees, they will go to the showroom to get the car.

Seyyid listened to the whole story of scholarship forum and the way it announced car prize for Asad. He knew Asad's family very well. Asad's father would often come to his lecture. Once or twice a year, Seyyid used to visit their house on invitation to give a lecture there. He smiled and said to Asad that he should not worry and go to the showroom and get the car. Inform me if there is any problem or you feel uncomfortable. They all left thanking Seyyid for his advice.

They all reached the showroom. On their way, Asad bought some sweets to give to Mr. Qadir. He was waiting for Asad. They all were shocked to see that the car given in prize to Asad was a brand new Japanese car. Asad's youngest sister selected the color and everybody agreed. However, Asad said to Mr. Qadir that he would like to call the sponsors of this scholarship. Mr. Qadir said that they will call you soon. They called him last night to tell you that you should not worry about their identity and profession. They are sponsoring this prize for intelligent students like you for the past several years. Asad asked for their phone number. This number was different from what he had. He noted it. Mr. Qadir prepared the documents and took his signatures and then gave them to Asad. He asked Asad if he had a driving license. Asad replied that he knew how to drive and has the license. They all left. While in car, Asad called Seyyid and informed him of the car and the situation. Seyyid prayed for him and told him not to worry. He also asked Asad to inform his close friends who come to Seyyid's house of the car prize. Asad did so and everyone wrote back, congratulating him. Yusuf also wrote and added that he was far away in another city and will return after a few days.

Asad called the phone number given to him by Mr. Qadir. However, he got a message that this number didn't exist anymore. He resent his email and it was returned back with a message that his email could not be delivered. He tried to use some techniques to trace back the source of email. However, the IP address was in USA, where none of his friends or relatives live. He then went to Seyyid's house and informed him of all of these developments. Seyyid patiently listened and then advised him to call his supervisor, Prof. Hameed. 'I am sure he knows the sponsors,' said Seyyid. Asad called Prof. Hameed and after Salams, asked him about the sponsors of the car award. 'You are not the first student to receive this award. I have had several students who have won awards from unknown sponsors,' he said to Asad. Asad then conveyed Seyyid's Salams to the professor. Prof. Hameed wanted to talk to Seyyid. Asad gave the phone to Seyyid. Prof. Hameed said Salams in return and praised him for his ethical training. He held Seyyid in high regards and said that Asad always speaks about him. Then he said to Seyyid: 'Respected Seyyid, this car award is given to Asad by someone who knows you too and comes to your classes. I am telling you this because you are their teacher. However, that person who called twice never disclosed his name and also wanted this to remain a secret. I request you to kindly not inform Asad.' He then said goodbye to Seyyid.

After the conversation was over, Seyyid didn't say anything about it to Asad. He just smiled and said to Asad that he should not worry about the identity of the sponsor as Prof. Hameed told him that so many intelligent students get awards and gifts from unknown sponsors. Asad was however, not pleased with it but he didn't say anything. Seyyid knew his expression and so he smiled at Asad and then asked him to pray two *rak'at* prayers to thank God for this gift. He then asked him to come on Saturday as he will give a dinner. 'I will try to find who the sponsor is for you,' he said. He asked him to come about thirty minutes earlier before *zuhr* as he had some special task for him and his brothers. Asad thanked him but was also surprised....

On Saturday, after *maghrib* prayers, Seyyid as usual sat on his seat to start his lecture. By that time, almost everyone close to Seyyid knew about the car gift given to Asad by an unknown sponsor and also Seyyid's approval of it. He said: 'Our today's topic is 'putting one's trust in God which is also known as *tawakkul.*' He then recited a verse of Qur'an:

فَإِذَا عَزَمْتَ فَتَوَكَّلْ عَلَى اللَّهِ ۚ إِنَّ اللَّهَ يُحِبُّ الْمُتَوَكِّلِينَ...

'*... then place your trust in Allah; surely Allah loves those who trust (Him)'* [3: 159].

He explained the meaning of *tawakkul* in practical life and how it affects human being's thinking and protects a person from anxiety, stress, feeling of helplessness and depression. 'Those who trust God are psychologically strong because they know that the All-powerful God is with them and can do anything for them. Thus, if they suffer any hardship or difficult circumstances or lose something valuable, they, even though become sad for a while, do not lose hope because of their trust in God's power. A lot of psychological problems in our society are because of lack of *tawakkul.*' He continued and everyone was totally absorbed in his words...

As the dinner started, Seyyid looked for Asad and whispered something to him. They all sat together, including Seyyid's close students. They were all talking about Asad's gift and its anonymity. Seyyid said to them not to worry about it as this is a way to do good and avoid becoming known. Asad said that he was now going to university with his new car and his brothers and sisters are also going together with him. Asad then came close to Seyyid and whispered something in his ear. Seyyid smiled and said nothing.

After the dinner was over, people started leaving one by one. Seyyid asked Yusuf and Asad to stay. Yusuf was surprised. Seyyid smiled and asked Yusuf to come closer to him so that no one would listen to their conversation. He then asked Yusuf if he knew about the gift given to Asad by some unknown sponsor. Yusuf replied: 'Respected Seyyid, I know that a car is given to brother Asad for his top research proposal. I am an MBA student and I don't know about PhD level research on computers.' Seyyid smiled and asked him: 'So you don't know anything about it?' He replied: 'Seyyid I was away at my auntie's house in another city when this all happened. I have just returned last night.' Seyyid then asked him why his car was different. He replied: 'Seyyid today I have brought my sister's Toyota car as my own car was not in a good shape after the long trip. I have given it for service. It is the same car as before.' Seyyid smiled at him and then prayed for both Asad and Yusuf. He then said to Asad to forget about the sponsors. He said: 'The person who has done this good deed is very smart. You may never be able to find him.' They all then left thanking Seyyid.

Joint project I - Dowry

It was three months before Shahid's sister's marriage. One of Seyyid's students, who belonged to a very well-off family got a mobile phone message from another such student. 'Brother, you know that Shahid's sister is getting married after three months. Today I heard his father talking to Seyyid that the preparations are under way. He asked Seyyid to pray that all goes well as the expectations of the family of the groom are high. So I think before Seyyid plans to ask anyone to help them, let's do our duty and be faster to reach them out without their knowledge.' 'I agree, but let us set basic rules for this 'special task'. In my view, though we know each other but we should have new mobile numbers specifically for it which should not be shared with anybody, even our own family members. Second, we will never write any names during our written communication. We will not call each other and finally we will discard our new SIM cards once the 'job' is done.' They agreed. 'If the first project goes well, we will do another project. I know that someone close to Seyyid requires a house and perhaps we can involve another brother from the group to contribute,' he said. 'Yes, agreed.' Next day, they bought new SIM cards and started their 'special task'. 'Let us try plan A first and see what happens. If it doesn't work then we will try plan B,' wrote one of them. They agreed. 'Keep your eyes and ears open and control your expressions. Seyyid is very smart and fast.'

'Mother! God has accepted your prayers. See this advertisement poster. I think the problem of my sister's dowry is solved, *insha'Allah*,' said Shahid. Just a minute ago, he had left for university and but then came back. He had seen a small poster that was under the main gate of his apartment complex and took it to his mother. Several of these posters were also posted on the wall outside. It read: Dowry in easy installments.

Just pay one installment and get the whole dowry. Pay no interest, best products in the market for your daughter's marriage …. Shahid's mother was very happy. 'Thank god,' she said. Shahid's sister's marriage was to take place after three months and the family, because of their poor financial situation, was not able to buy several items for her dowry. They were only able to buy some minor jewelry and dresses for her. Shahid's father was a retired school teacher and he used to tutor students. Shahid had two sisters and one brother – all younger than him. Shahid's mother noted the phone and address of the shop and decided to go there with him on the coming Thursday.

'Sister, look at this refrigerator, you may like it, it's a new brand and the best model we have,' said the shopkeeper. 'But this refrigerator and all these items you have shown are very expensive,' said Shahid's mother. The shopkeeper smiled and replied: 'Actually all these items are expensive if you buy them individually or separate. But if you take our special deal for dowry and fill the form that we have announced on our website and publicity posters, you will get special concession and will have to pay in easy installments without any interest.' Shahid and his sister were also actively looking at different items with their mother and he said to his mother: 'Mother, he is a good marketer, he is offering this scheme so that a lot of people will buy bulk items for the dowry of their daughters and so he will earn more profit by selling more. Let us see the deal he is offering for dowry items. Then we can decide.' Shahid's mother agreed.

They both then went to the manager's room and filled the special dowry offer form. It asked their address, contact number, ID card copy and presented a list of items and their models from the shop's showcase and catalogue as well as the conditions for the installments. According to it, they could pay a very small amount in the beginning and then pay the first installment after six months. Shahid filled the form and told his mother about the installment. She was happy to know that the maximum time for the first installment was after six months. ‘We can arrange some money until that time,’ she said. ‘Let us select the items and fill the form,’ she continued.

For the next three hours, Shahid, his sister and his mother were in the shop and selected almost all the items required for the dowry. The total amount was huge and they took easy installment scheme that would allow them to pay back during the next three years with a small down payment amount. While they were waiting for the manager to come, the salesman come towards them and said that they have another scheme for jewelry, if they want to buy. Shahid asked him to bring the offer. He gave a form that had jewelry offer, but it was conditional. It was valid only with the other items. The installments were easy and again the maximum time for the first one was six months. Shahid’s mother and sister wanted to see the quality of the jewelry first and then fill the form and take the deal.

They then went to the jewelry section and found that the quality and variety was good. They selected one complete set for her and then asked Shahid to fill the form. After that, they went to the manager’s room. He took the form and made some calculations and then said: ‘Sister, we will offer you an overall 25% concession because you are also buying the jewelry. The amount seems to be big but in easy installments it will not be a problem. We will also provide free delivery of all the items to any address in the city. If you agree, please sign and write your names here on these two forms.’ Shahid signed it and then gave the forms back. ‘We will make one copy for you and give it to you now. Kindly just call us whenever you need any item. You may need jewelry earlier like many of our customers. Please let us know and we will deliver it to your home through our special service,’ he said. They thanked the shopkeeper and took the copy of the deal and went back home.

Shahid’s sister’s marriage took place without any problems. All of their friends helped them according to their time and capacity and Seyyid recited the *nikah* for her. As a surprise, a lot of gifts were given by Seyyid's students and lecture attendees to Shahid's sister and her husband. These were enough to pay all the loans they had taken for her marriage and dowry expenses. On the Saturday after their marriage, Seyyid especially invited the bride, the groom and their families to his house with a special dinner from his side. Seyyid gave a very good and inspiring lecture on 'merits and *thawab* of night prayers.'

Seyyid explained why night prayers are important, especially when they are performed right before the time of *fajr* prayers. 'Night prayer is like a shield. If a person offers night prayers, he is protected the next day. But then, night prayer has to be recited with a proper method and one has to understand the reason for its merits. If you ponder over the last *rak'at* of night prayer, you will see that the recommended supplications are so awakening and inspiring for one's soul. Additionally, the person who offers night prayers, ponders over his deeds and intentions during last 24 hours and then repents for his sins that he has committed during that time which means that he becomes more vigilant over himself, his memory becomes sharp, the quality of his good intentions and actions becomes better day by day and so does the avoidance of sins by him. Similarly, he prays for the wellbeing and forgiveness of at least forty good people which means that he develops more respect and love towards them and becomes a socially active person.' Finally, Seyyid said that it is recommended that one should recite the last *ruku'* (section) of *Surah Hashr* [*Surah* no. 59] of Holy Qur'an and ponder over its meanings as it is very beneficial. Everybody listened to the inspiring lecture of Seyyid with great interest to the point that nobody moved from their place. Seyyid then recited *du'a* for the newly married couple and asked everyone to recite *salawat*. After dinner, he gave special gifts to the newly married couple. They all thanked him and left.

Shahid's exams were over now and like his father, he also tutored younger students to pay the first installment of the dowry. Although they had some money from the gifts, the amount was not sufficient. He was regular in his attendance at Seyyid's house and sometimes, Seyyid would ask him about his studies and the work he was doing and his plans for future. Shahid would tell Seyyid what he was preparing his thesis defense viva which was due in the next four weeks and that he wanted to go abroad to pursue his doctorate in Spiritual Psychology. Seyyid prayed for his success and was surprised that this new discipline exists. Shahid said that it is a new discipline and he wishes to do research on Spiritual Psychology from the Islamic point of view, especially on the prayers and *munajat* that are mentioned in the book *Mafatih al Jinan* and observe their effects on various aspects of a person's psychology and behavior. Seyyid was impressed. 'My MSc thesis is also on scientific study of effects of a prayer of Imam Zayn al Abedin (as) on depression in a few patients,' he continued. Seyyid knew about his thesis topic before and so he asked about the results. Shahid said that he found positive effects on depressed patients and compared his results with the patients taking antidepressant medicines.' Seyyid said: '*Masha Allah*, God bless you.' However, it was apparent that Shahid had no financial support for pursuing his PhD abroad and so he didn't say anything else to keep his self-respect. After a few seconds, Seyyid said to him in a very thoughtful tone: 'I want you to present your thesis work here in our gathering after you have successfully defended it.' Shahid agreed and requested to Seyyid to pray for him and then left.

'Excuse me, what?' Shahid's mother said in surprise to the shop manager. 'Madam, thanks for the payment of the remaining amount that you made three months ago. You don't have any balance amount to pay to us. I am sorry we didn't send a letter of thanks from our shop to your address,' replied the shopkeeper explaining the reason for his thanks earlier. 'But we haven't paid any amount,' she replied. 'Maybe your son has paid and you have no information. Please ask him. If there are any further queries or information required by you, kindly ask him to come to our shop,' he said. Shahid's mother thought that there is perhaps a mistake in their record keeping or maybe there is an error in their computer records as they hadn't paid any amount. She had called the shop one day before the due date to ask about their preferred mode of payment, either cash or by check and the reply shocked her. She then waited for Shahid to come back home from university. When she informed Shahid about it, he too thought that there was a mistake in the shop's computer records and so he decided to go to the shop the next day with cash and pay it right there.

At 10 am, Shahid reached the shop with the copy of the deal they were given before. The shop manager looked into his records and then said that his mother called yesterday and that he had informed her about the payment made by your family. 'Look at this sir, this is our computer record. Someone paid us the entire remaining amount in cash three months ago,' he said. 'But we have no information about it,' replied Shahid. 'Do you have records of his name or address or contact number?' he asked. 'Yes we do. Let me print it out for you. We also gave Mr. Hamid, the person who paid the amount, a receipt of the payment,' said the shop manager. He then gave a printout to Shahid that had the address and phone number of Mr. Hamid.

Shahid thanked the shop manager and came out of the shop. He called the number. 'Hello, who is this?' A female voice answered. Shahid said that he wanted to talk to Mr. Hamid. 'Excuse me this is a surgery ward of City hospital, whom do you want to talk to? Do you know the bed number of Mr. Hamid?' said the lady who was apparently a nurse. Shahid immediately realized that as the money was paid three months ago it may not be possible for Mr. Hamid to be here now. 'No thanks,' he said and then hang up the phone. He then took a taxi to find the house of Mr. Hamid.

After 30 minutes, Shahid reached the given address and found that it was a tutoring center in a bungalow. He went inside and asked about Mr. Hamid and found that there was nobody there by that name. 'Excuse me, was anyone employed here three months ago by the name of Hamid or a person previously employed by this name and left your center three months ago?' he asked. The head of the center said that no one with this name was ever employed or left his center during the last two years. Shahid then left and called his mother to inform her about what had happened at the shop and his efforts to find Mr. Hamid. He then left for Seyyid's house as it was near *zuhr* prayers.

Seyyid attentively listened to the whole story of dowry, its scheme, payment and then about the phone and address of this unknown person, Mr. Hamid. 'What should I do now Seyyid?' asked Shahid. Seyyid replied that he should pray for that person who has done this good deed to him. 'You should also pray two *rak'ats* of thanks to God and also for that person and remember him in your prayers,' he told Shahid. 'Whatever you order Seyyid,' Shahid replied. 'And remember do not tell anyone here about it. You should keep your self-respect. Now you can pay full attention to your thesis defense and also remember that after completing it, you have to give a presentation on it here,' reminded Seyyid. 'Yes, I will do that,' replied Shahid.

Seyyid then remembered the unknown typewritten letter he had received a few weeks ago that had only one sentence: 'Salaam Respected Seyyid, first project completed successfully.' He didn't mention this to Shahid.

Then, they performed their prayers and Shahid left for his home and informed his mother and father and other family members. They were all very happy and thanked God and then offered prayers of thanks and also prayer for that unknown person who had bought the dowry and jewelry.

Joint project II - House

It was 11 am in the morning. The bell rang and Bilal looked out from his room's window, surprised to see the postman in front of his home. Bilal hurriedly came out and took the big envelope and signed in the receipt book. The postman left on his bike and Bilal came up in his room. He then opened the envelope and found a letter and a small envelope inside it. He was surprised to read the letter. It read:

'Dear Mr. Bilal, I am a friend of Mr. Habib who is the uncle of your very close friend Mobin. He lives in Canada Mr. Habib asked me to purchase a house as a gift for Mobin's family. Mobin's mother is Mr. Habib's sister. Since last several years, their relationship is not good due to minor disagreements between Mobin's father and Mr. Habib and so they have no communication now. Because he is currently very sick, he felt very lonely and wanted to give this gift so that the two families start communication again and forgive each other. Once he recovers, he will come here and meet Mobin and his family. He is currently under intense treatment and so is not responding to his phone. However, his son may reply to emails. The address is: <...@.....>. As per his instructions, I have purchased the house with 4 bedrooms and a small yard and the ownership papers and the keys of the house are in the small envelope. Kindly give it to Mobin's family and explain to them the situation in the best possible way you can. I fully trust you.

'Mr. Habib's friend'

Bilal then noticed that there was no sender's address on the big envelope. It was a bit surprising for him. He was puzzled as to how he can give this to Mobin. Mobin was a regular attendee of Seyyid's lectures and he never mentioned to anyone his family's financial difficulties. Sometimes, Mobin's sister and brother would also come to Seyyid's lectures. He was one of the brightest students close to completing his masters in biotechnology in the highest-ranked university of the country. He had ambitions of going abroad for his PhD but his family's financial situation and home responsibilities were making him uncertain about his future. He was usually quiet in gatherings. He and Bilal used to exchange few formal sentences. Not knowing exactly what to do, Bilal immediately called Seyyid to help him. Seyyid told him that he should ask Mobin to come over and first talk to him about his uncle and then inform him about the house given as a gift. He also told Bilal not to ask Mobin about his family's financial condition. 'Behave as if you don't know anything. Inform me if you have any difficulty,' he said. Bilal thanked Seyyid and then called Mobin. He was busy in writing his thesis. Bilal told him that it was urgent and gave him his home address.

Mobin came and Bilal welcomed him. He was very sober in his manners and wouldn't talk much. Bilal asked him about his studies and preparations for his thesis. Then, Bilal slowly asked him if he had any relatives outside living outside the country. Mobin mentioned about a maternal uncle named Habib living in Canada. But then, when Bilal asked where he was now, Mobin said that they don't have any relations with him and have no news of him for the past 10 years. Bilal was surprised. Then he mentioned that uncle Habib has sent a gift for his family from Canada through his friend. Mobin was shocked to hear this and thought Bilal was joking. Bilal explained to him that since his uncle is very sick, he remembers you all very much and he asked his friend to buy a house for your family and sent the ownership papers and keys with a friend.

Bilal brought tea and some snacks for Mobin and then he gave the envelope to Mobin who was still in a state of shock and surprise and said: 'I don't know if my mother and father will take this gift or not.' Bilal replied: 'Remember Mobin, few weeks ago Seyyid spoke about *sileye rahmi*, keeping relations and doing goodness to your relatives and its *thawab*. One of the things Seyyid emphasized was that it prolongs one's life. Now if your mother and father accept this gift, it will probably have healing effect on your uncle's recovery from illness and may prolong his life.' Mobin agreed. 'You should remind your parents of what Seyyid said and then convince them in the best way, Mobin.' Bilal further persuaded him and told Mobin that he has already informed Seyyid about it. Finally, after few minutes of discussions and sharing ideas, Mobin thanked Bilal and left. Bilal called Seyyid and told him about it.

In the evening, Mobin, his sister, brother and his parents were with Seyyid. They came about an hour before *maghrib* prayers to discuss the situation and whether to take the house gift or not. 'You must take this gift with good intention and create a room in your heart for him. Forget minor differences. Even if in your view he has done something wrong, you must forgive him. How will you ask forgiveness from God on the Day of Judgment when you are not willing to forget minor mistakes of your brother? Keeping good relations doesn't mean only calling each other. Your uncle has taken the first step towards good relationship by sending the gift. You should not break his heart. You should respond positively and accept it. It may prolong his life. Don't you want that?' he asked Mobin's mother. 'Yes I do, Seyyid,' she replied.

Seyyid then looked towards Mobin's father and with his powerful convincing style, persuaded him to forgive Mr. Habib and asked him to write him an email and also pray for him and give *sadaqa* (charity) for his quick and complete recovery from sickness. He also asked Mobin's mother to pray for her brother and ask God to unite him with her family as soon as possible. They all promised to Seyyid that they will forget all the past disputes, pray for him and welcome him.

They then prayed *maghrib* prayers and attended his lecture which was on prejudice or *assabiyyah*. He explained different types of prejudice and their devastating effects on one's life, thinking, the society and finally, the hereafter. 'A person suffering from prejudice of any kind is like a blind individual. He cannot see anything that has human quality because prejudice removes humanity from his eyes. He behaves like an animal. He supports others not because they are on truth and justice but because they are of his tribe, family, group and his fellows from his own race. He cannot see justice and so will harm someone innocent or someone on truth who deserves justice. That person can commit murder or any other crime against innocent person or people. This is the reason that Imam Sadiq (as) has said that 'A person who has prejudice in his heart to the size of a mustard seed will not even smell paradise'', he said. Everyone sitting in the lecture was shocked and terrified to listen to Seyyid's words. After lecture, they had dinner as usual and thanked Seyyid and left.

Mobin's family moved into the new house soon afterwards. They also wrote an email to his son and thanked his father for the house gift. They received a reply which didn't mention anything besides the news of Mr. Habib's recovery. A few weeks later, they got an email that there will be another surprise for them soon. All of Mobin's family members were waiting for him now…

Four weeks later, Seyyid's home bell rang. When Seyyid came out, he found an aged, frail man, well dressed and he looked like he had come from a Western country. He introduced himself as Mr. Habib and he said to Seyyid that he came last time to his house 10 years ago and had attended a few of his lectures. Seyyid immediately welcomed him inside his house's yard and asked him about his health and told him that he knew about his sickness and recovery through Mobin. Mr. Habib said that he left for Canada and due to some family issues with the Mobin's father, he was forced to cutoff relations with them. Seyyid carefully listened. 'I have now come to you for guidance and for mediation Seyyid. They all accept you. Although they have forgiven me as I read in the email but I want to make sure that it is true. Whatever you say, they will agree upon. If you ask them to forgive me, they will. Seyyid please help me. I do not want to be away from my sister because of her husband's enmity towards me. I want Mobin to study abroad. He is a very intelligent boy,' he pleaded. Seyyid promised him that he will do so. He asked him where he was staying. Mr. Habib said that he was staying at his old friend's house. Then Seyyid asked him: 'Did you send the gift of house for Mobin's family?' Mr. Habib said 'No Seyyid. It's a total surprise for me. I never sent them any gift. Rather I have brought few gifts for them with me.'

Seyyid was surprised at first and then thought for a while and told Mr. Habib that he should not mention it to Mobin's family and behave as if he has given the gift of new house to them. But then he should pay equal or more amount of money or spend it in gifts for them. Mr. Habib agreed. He said that he will take Mobin with him for his studies. Seyyid said: 'That's the best. But you should send him back to his own country. I will also ask him to do the same,' Seyyid asked if he brought his family with him. He said that his wife, son and daughter are with him. Then Seyyid asked him to come with his family to his house about an hour before *maghrib* that day in the evening. He would like to talk with them before they all met Mobin's family. Mr. Habib thanked him and left. Seyyid then went inside his house and talked to his wife about this issue and told her a few important things. He then called Mobin and asked him to come with all his family members at *maghrib* prayers.

As soon as Mr. Habib and his family reached Seyyid's house, an hour before *maghrib*, Seyyid came to the door and guided them inside. Mr. Habib and his son sat with him. Few other students were also there. Bilal then asked Seyyid about how can good family relationships keep a person healthy. Seyyid started with findings from modern research that has shown that people who have peaceful family life live longer and do not suffer from major psychological as well as physical illnesses, as those who live with stress such as the ones who live alone, or are divorced or have stressful relationships with their immediate relatives. This is because psychosocial stress is a well-known factor for heart diseases, diabetes, problems of sleep that itself leads to several other problems. Imagine you have a family relative with whom your relations are not good. Every time you think of him, you will be stressed. However, imagine if the same person again enjoys good relationship, seeing his relative or even thinking of him will lead to relaxation and happiness. Then, Seyyid said that he will continue this topic in his lecture that night.

The time for *maghrib* prayers was approaching and people started coming. Mr. Habib and his son started to do their *wuzu* and started interacting with other people. Just before the prayer began, Mobin, his brother and father also came to join the prayers. They didn't recognize Mr. Habib and his son. His mother and sister went into the ladies' section. There, inside Seyyid's house, Mobin's mother was surprised to see Mr. Habib's wife and his daughter after so many years. They all met and then because the prayer was going to start, they got ready for it. They were all very happy.

After prayers, Seyyid gave a very inspiring lecture on Family Relationship from Qur'an and Islamic traditions. It was a very inspiring lecture. Everybody was just stunned by the importance of family relations and rights of family members upon each other and the *thawab* of keeping good relations and helping each other in the time of need. They didn't move until Seyyid's lecture was over. At the end of his lecture, Seyyid welcomed Mr. Habib and introduced him. Everyone including Mobin and his father welcomed him. Mobin's father also hugged him and they met like brothers. Seyyid smiled while looking at them and asked them to sit near him. Soon, the dinner started and they sat beside one another. Finally, when everyone left Seyyid gathered the two families around him and talked to them. Mobin's mother then met her brother and talked with him and her nephew, she was full of joy and happiness. Seyyid asked them to thank God for this blessing for all of them. They were all nice in behavior and respected each other. Then Mr. Habib said that because Seyyid 'ordered' me, I have another small gift for my sister and her family. 'I will take

Mobin with me for his higher education. I know that he is finishing his MSc thesis and I will take him for his doctorate and post doctorate with me. Of course, on one condition and that is, he will come back here and serve his own society.' Mobin was overjoyed and so was his mother, but his father's facial expression showed disagreement. But then Seyyid said to him: 'You forgot what I mentioned in my lecture today!' Finally, he agreed and they all then started coming out in the yard of Seyyid's house.

When they were leaving, Mobin's mother was very happy. She wanted to talk to Seyyid separately in private and so Seyyid and his wife took her on one side. She thanked Seyyid and his wife and told them that she was extremely happy to see her brother's family after so many years.

They all then said goodbye to Seyyid and left together.

Seyyid then went inside his house and thanked his wife for her role in reuniting the two families. But he was thinking…who had bought that house for Mobin's family…. For a moment, he thought it was Bilal. But then he smiled and dismissed the idea.

A few days later, Seyyid got an envelope pasted on the inside of the gate of his yard. He opened it and found one sentence written in it:

'Respected Seyyid, with the grace of God and your training and help, the project was completed successfully. Many, many thanks.'

Seyyid smiled and thanked God.

*****

Well arranged marriage and...

Qamar was with his mother and sister in the big city bazaar for shopping early one morning on Sunday. When they were inside the large food supermarket, his mother saw Seyyid with his son of about 12 years of age and informed Qamar and his sister. This was the first time they had seen Seyyid outside his home and shopping. They stopped their own shopping and watched him stealthily carrying his own half-filled trolley. They followed him slowly and looked at him from a distance to see how he selected items.

They saw that he would sometimes use his mobile to talk to someone and then put the thing in the trolley. Sometimes, he would talk with his son. At other times, he would speak very softly with the salesman. He was careful in selecting a product before he decided to buy it. They were impressed by his sober and graceful manners. Finally, they decided to give Seyyid a surprise....

They went near him and said Salams together. Seyyid replied with a graceful manner and was surprised. Seyyid asked his son to say Salams to all of them. He was a bit shy and said it very softly. Qamar's mother smiled and took him near her and started talking with him, asking what grade was he. Qamar then introduced his sister. Seyyid said: 'Yes I remember Samana very well. The highly ambitious chemistry student. Am I right?' Seyyid said it with a meaningful style. 'Yes Seyyid. I have just given BSc exams and I am waiting for my results and after that I want to pursue higher studies abroad. Please pray for me,' she said. Seyyid replied: 'Yes. May God bless you with success. Are you reciting the *du'a* from *Sahifaye*

Sajjadiya that I advised you a few months ago?' She replied in affirmative.

Seyyid continued: 'You are very talented like Qamar. But remember that there are more difficult exams in life than studying chemistry. I think you are capable of achieving much more valuable things in your life.' She asked immediately: 'Seyyid, I don't get what you mean.' Seyyid looked at her and Qamar and then calmly said: 'Perhaps after your results you may know what I mean.' Then Seyyid asked them all to come to his house next Saturday and said goodbye to them and left the shop after payment. They also finished their shopping quickly and saw in the parking lot that Seyyid left in an old car and were very much surprised to see him driving it.

'Seyyid, my thesis defense was excellent, *alhamdolillah*,' Shahid called him from his mobile phone after he was declared successful in MSc thesis defense. He scored near perfect grades with distinction. He then called Seyyid and continued... 'I am bringing sweets Seyyid. I will reach within an hour.' Seyyid asked him to first go to his house and say thanks to his parents and buy sweets for them and then come to his house. He thanked Seyyid for this advice.

Near *maghrib*, Shahid reached Seyyid's house with sweets. Seyyid asked him to keep it and distribute it after prayers. Then they performed their prayers. Seyyid gave a very inspiring short lecture on merits of seeking knowledge. He said that knowledge is the base for all good actions a person does. However, knowledge is a tool to worship God, it is not the aim. That's why it is *wajib* or obligatory so that we all worship God using our knowledge. Relieving suffering of human beings by doing research is one of the best forms of knowledge.

After prayers, Seyyid told the small gathering that *mashaAllah* Shahid has defended his thesis today with distinction and so he has brought sweets. Then, he prayed for Shahid's success and recited *salawat*. Other close students were also present and they congratulated Shahid. Then, Seyyid made an announcement: 'On Saturday, I will not give my lecture as I usually do. Shahid will present his research and we will listen to him,' he said. 'Please inform your friends and family members also, as the topic he is going to present is important for all of us,' he said. They all then left slowly, talking with Shahid and asking questions about his research and future plans. Seyyid was carefully watching who was talking to Shahid.....

On Saturday, Shahid arrived at Seyyid's house with his laptop and borrowed a projector and a screen as Seyyid wanted him to present in such a way that everybody would be able to see his slides and listen to him. Soon, people started arriving and all his friends came with their families. Seyyid started prayers and then, he asked few students to help people sit in such a way that everyone would be able to watch Shahid's lecture on screen.

The ladies were also sitting in the yard with a partition so that they could be comfortable. Shahid set the screen and computer with microphone and asked Seyyid's permission to start. First, Seyyid spoke a few words of high praise for Shahid. He said: '*MashaAllah*, we have such a talented young, well-mannered, sober and very pious *momin* like Shahid who has done very valuable research on one of the prayers of Imam Zayn al Abedin (as) and scientifically proved that it had very significant effect on depression. He got his MSc with distinction and has submitted his research paper in a top journal. Shahid has a bright future and I pray for his success.' Then, he asked Shahid to begin his lecture.

Shahid started with presenting some general information on depression as to how common it was in the society. He then presented his research, why he selected a *du'a* of Imam Zayn al Abedin (as) which he used to pray in the time of difficulty. He also talked about how he selected and evaluated patients with depression, how he requested the patients to participate in the study, tested their stress related hormones, checked their heart rates and parameters of depression and how he proved that that the patients who listened to *du'a* regularly significantly recovered much better and faster than those who were taking anti-depressant medicines.

He then said: 'Our research clearly shows that if people recite *du'a* on a daily basis, they will never suffer from stress and depression.' When his lecture finished, everyone recited *salawat* and many voices of *mashaAllah* and *subhanAllah* were heard from the audience. Then, Shahid said if anyone had questions. Seyyid asked a question: 'Dear Shahid, tell me if you didn't get the significant results, would that mean that the *du'a* had no effect?' Shahid intelligently replied: 'No Seyyid. It would mean that our experiment was not designed properly. We would then test the *du'a* with a better experimental design.' Everyone was surprised at the extempore answer given by Shahid. Seyyid said: '*MashaAllah*, great answer.' Then few questions were asked from both ladies and gents' sections. Finally, one question was asked from ladies: 'Mr. Shahid, what are your future plans for research?' Shahid said that he wished to pursue PhD in Spiritual Psychology abroad and work on other *du'as*, especially some of the *du'as* of Imam Zayn al Abedin (as) and Imam Ali (as). 'If God wishes, I will do this type of research which is a new area in experimental and spiritual psychology for the propagation of Islam. I have already told Seyyid about it,' he replied.

Seyyid then asked Shahid his final question: 'Dear Shahid, I am asking you a personal question. I know you are not married. What do you expect from your wife-to-be?' Shahid was a bit shy and looked down and then said: 'Seyyid, this is a difficult question. If I do research, I would like my wife to support my research and make home life suitable for it so that we can serve Islam more by doing this type of research.' Seyyid said that it was difficult to find such an educated and believing wife who would sacrifice her career for him. 'Shahid, dear you are looking for an educated *momina* to support your research. It's almost impossible. But God will help you.' Then he asked everyone to recite a *salawat* and pray for Shahid.

After the lecture, all of the guests had food. Shahid was at the center, everyone was congratulating him and asking him questions. Some of his friends had brought gifts for him. Seyyid was closely watching who was meeting and talking with Shahid. Finally, after dinner, people started leaving. Seyyid said goodbye to everyone. Seyyid sat for a while on his seat when he was all alone and thanked God for his help.

On Tuesday morning at 10, Seyyid's house bell rang. Qamar's mother was there. Seyyid immediately went to the gate and welcomed her. Seyyid asked his wife to take her inside. Then, he asked if everything was okay as this was unusual of her to come like that. 'Seyyid, I want your advice on an important issue,' she said. Seyyid requested her to be comfortable and talk without any fear or hesitation. She said: 'Seyyid as you know, we all came here on Saturday to attend Shahid's lecture. I really liked that young man. His manners were so humble. He was brilliant and his future and his reply about married life really impressed me. Samana has been also talking highly of him. I know my daughter very well. I think she is inclined towards him but she is too shy to say it.' Seyyid was attentively listening to her. He said: 'It is possible. However, your daughter wants to study chemistry abroad. Remember last week that's what she told me in the bazaar.' Qamar's mother said that it is possible that she took your words seriously that there are higher levels of good deeds that intelligent persons like her can achieve. 'Remember Seyyid you challenged her. Perhaps she has accepted a difficult challenge to marry a person like Shahid and support his research for the sake of Islam and give up something she loved to study as an aim of her life,' she replied.

Seyyid smiled meaningfully. He then said: 'Shahid is a very good person. If Samana marries him, that would be very good. They both will have a good productive life to serve Islam.

Insha'Allah. But Shahid doesn't belong to a rich family. He cannot afford his PhD.' Shahid's mother said: 'Shahid is like my own son. Even if they don't marry, I give you my word that we will support his studies because his research will benefit Islam. I will ask Qamar to start supporting him so that he prepares for his PhD.' Seyyid replied: 'Thanks, May God bless you. But please don't tell Qamar to talk to Shahid directly about support as this will hurt his self-respect and I would not recommend it.' She agreed. Seyyid then asked her to talk to her daughter about Shahid and then if she agrees, talk to Qamar about it and then if he agrees, they all should inform him and come to see him. She agreed and thanked Seyyid for his wise advice.

Two days later, Seyyid received a call early in the morning from Qamar's mother that her daughter has agreed and so has Qamar and they want to see him. Seyyid told them to come over the next day. He then called Shahid and asked him to come over with his mother. Shahid came with his mother about an hour before *zuhr*. Seyyid guided them to his living room and then they sat together. Seyyid's wife brought tea for them.

Then Seyyid told them about a marriage proposal for Shahid. Seyyid said: 'I have selected a good bride for your son. I know that Shahid will agree with my choice.' Shahid immediately said: 'Yes Seyyid. Your choice is an honor for me.' Shahid's mother also said: 'Thank you Seyyid. But we are not so well-off, who will support my son for his studies and if he goes abroad, he will not be able to take his wife.' Seyyid smiled and calmly said: 'God has accepted your prayers. Everything is arranged for your son. Then he told them that he has selected a good family and if they agree, he will propose for Shahid. They asked a few questions and when Shahid came to know that it was Qamar's sister, he was a bit shy and concerned. 'But Seyyid, they are very rich. I don't have money to study abroad and take my wife with me. We don't have the high class expensive living that they have. I am sure Qamar's sister will not be happy with us. We will also feel belittled when they will come to our apartment and when we will visit their expensive big villa. I will not be able to provide my wife with the living facilities which she has now. Our life is very simple. We live in an apartment.' he said. Seyyid listened patiently and said that in Islam, the criterion for marriage is faith and piety, nothing else. 'You should not feel inferior. You will have to respect her and try your best to make her life comfortable. Remember that it is an honor for them that a believer like you will be their son-in-law and an honor for you that a good, believing and intelligent girl will be your wife who will support you.'

Then, he told Shahid's mother that she has to treat her bride like her own daughter and give her respect. 'The respect you will give her is because of her faith and she will do the same. Faith is much more valuable than money and material possessions and it is tested in difficult situations. Your adjustment with her will be a test of your faith,' he explained. Shahid's mother then called his father and took his advice. He agreed. They then requested Seyyid to propose. Seyyid said he will do that and inform them when he gets a reply. They left thanking Seyyid.

Seyyid then called Qamar's mother and told her that he has contacted Shahid and his family and got their approval. 'They asked me to propose for your daughter,' he said. Qamar's mother was very happy. She said that her daughter wanted to talk to him on the phone. Seyyid then asked Qamar's mother, her daughter and Qamar to come to his house for a short visit as he wanted to talk to them. They asked his permission to come near *maghrib* but then Seyyid said that he didn't want anyone to see them so they should come around 3 pm. They agreed. Seyyid then told his wife a few things and got ready for them.

They arrived at 3 and Seyyid and his wife led them inside his living room. His wife brought tea and snacks for them.

Seyyid started talking to all of them about the differences between their life and Shahid and his family's life. 'Shahid, as you saw him, is a very pious and intelligent young man. His mother and father are more respectable as they brought him and his brother and sister up in a very noble manner, despite the fact that their life was simple and their earning were limited. They could have had a better life if they hadn't spent their money on their children's education. I am sure you have heard the story of Imam Husayn (as) giving a very big amount of money to a teacher who taught something very small to one of his sons. Knowledge with piety is the most valuable thing one can have and Shahid has it. You know that both of his parents were school teachers,' he continued. 'Yes Seyyid, I know Shahid very well since I started coming to your lectures about four years ago and became his friend,' said Qamar. 'So another dimension is added to your friendship and that is family relationship. You will surely give him and his family more respect and you will get it in reciprocation. Never let them feel that they have differences in financial status with yours. I am sure you are all well trained,' said Seyyid with a smile. 'It is all your training respected Seyyid,' said Qamar's mother. Samana was listening to Seyyid very attentively. Then, she said to Seyyid that she has left something valuable that she loved and that was her desire to get PhD in chemistry and pursue another path for the sake of Islam and help a good person like Shahid.

Seyyid prayed for her and then said: 'Good daughter, you are blessed to have such a good *momin* and intelligent husband. Thank God for this special favor and always support him. But you can still pursue your studies if it doesn't affect your home life. You will get much more *thawab*. You will manage home, support him and also continue your studies. But remember, your first priority is to support him with a peaceful home and your good manners.' 'Seyyid I am worried how Shahid will continue his studies. He must get a scholarship and that should be sufficient to support both of us,' she said of her concerns. Seyyid smiled and said: 'My daughter, God is great. He knows what's going on in the heart of his servants. The moment one determines to do a good action, help from God starts right there. I am sure Shahid will secure a very good scholarship for his PhD. You should also pray to God for his blessings.' While he was saying this, he quickly glanced at Qamar. Qamar knew what Seyyid meant and smiled faintly for a moment so that his sister and mother wouldn't notice. He then said that now he will proceed with informing Shahid and his family that you have accepted his proposal.

Next day, the families met at Seyyid's house and soon the date for *nikah* was fixed. As usual, Seyyid was very strict about simplicity in marriage. He chose 5 gold coins as *mehr* for the bride. After a few days, Shahid got a 'scholarship' for his studies and he then started filling his admission application to join a PhD program in Spiritual Psychology in a top university. Samana also decided to continue her MSc in chemistry in the same university as Shahid. He and Samana were married soon in a very simple manner and then started their new life together. They were planning to leave for their studies after a few months....

Seyyid thanked God for His special favors.....

Scholarship

'But Seyyid how is it possible? My son left three months ago on a scholarship from the Brilliant Trust to do his PhD abroad. You are aware of it. They took his interview on Skype. They gave him the scholarship money for the first year. And today, when I met the director of Brilliant Trust for the first time, he told me that my son was never interviewed by him. They don't have any record of him in their system. He has never received any money from them. Then who has paid him the scholarship money Seyyid?' said Rafiq's father. He was one of the attendees of Seyyid's lecture and his son was among the top students of the university in his MD exam. He then applied for PhD in Applied Nanotechnology and secured a 4-year scholarship from Brilliant Trust. Seyyid knew Rafiq very well as he used to come to his lectures and was friendly with almost all of the other students who used to come to Seyyid's lectures.

Seyyid suggested a simple solution. 'Ask your son the bank account from which money was transferred to his account. Then you will know who the person is.' Rafiq's father replied that his son and he himself had a joint local bank account and the scholarship money was deposited in that account. When he went to USA, he opened a bank account there and then this money was then transferred to his new account there. The amount was 1500 dollars per month and for one year, which means the total money is 18000 dollars. 'I have already informed Rafiq about this new discovery just now through my mobile. Tomorrow morning, I will go to the bank to find out the account number from where the money was deposited to our account three months ago. I am worried about the coming year. What if the person who has done doesn't deposit the money again, what will happen to my son's studies? That's why I have asked Rafiq to be frugal from now on and save some money.' Seyyid smiled and said that he should not worry, God will help. 'A person who has done this for the first time will definitely do it again,' he said calmly.

Next day, Rafiq's father went to the bank and met the bank manager and explained to him the situation and requested him to give the account details and the name of the account holder. The manager asked the relevant section to proceed with the request. However, he informed him that according to the bank rules, he was not authorized to give details of the customers or depositors. Anyway, after a few minutes, the manager looked at the file provided to him by the deposit section that someone deposited cash in dollars to their account three months ago. That person has written his name, mobile number and address as per requirements. 'I am sure that this person has provided incorrect information about himself. He wishes to keep himself unknown and wants to help your son's studies in this way. I am also sure that next time he will not come to this bank. He will probably use another method to give the scholarship money to your son. As you know, there are many ways to anonymously transfer money to a bank account. He can even open an account in my branch and legally put a restriction on us not to disclose his identity. If he knows the name and account number of your son there, he can also open an online bank account in any country and transfer money to your son and close the account after that,' he explained. Rafiq's father thanked him and left the bank.

At *zuhr* prayers the next day, he was talking to Seyyid about it and a few of Seyyid's students and others were listening and were surprised. 'Does your son have any close friend whom you think could have done it?' asked Shareef. 'No, all his friends are same; maybe someone else has done this great act of goodness. Almost all of his friends come here in Seyyid's lectures and are aware of this situation as Rafiq is writing to all of them about this new sponsor of scholarship,' replied his father. Seyyid was quietly watching the faces of his students and also listening to the conversation going on. He then said to Rafiq's father: 'How was Rafiq informed of the scholarship scheme for the first time? Did the Brilliant Trust call him or send an email or did he receive a letter or see the ad in the newspaper?' Rafiq's father replied: 'As far as I remember, it was an ad in the newspaper that Rafiq saw and showed me and then he applied for the scholarship and sent the required documents by post to them. Then they did a Skype interview with him and after about four weeks, he got a letter by post that he had been accepted for the scholarship. Although they told him that the results will be announced in two weeks but it took four weeks for the letter.' Seyyid then inquired about who knew in the family or friends of Rafiq about this scholarship and his application. 'As you know Seyyid, Rafiq is very social. I am sure he informed all of his friends about it.' Seyyid then asked him to bring all the letters from Brilliant Trust, especially the last letter of acceptance sent to him.

After two days, Rafiq's father brought the letters at *zuhr* prayers. Some students were very curious about this issue and were sitting near Seyyid. Then Seyyid saw the three letters and after a few minutes, he said that the logo of Brilliant Trust and the quality of letterhead paper were a bit different in the last letter. 'This means that someone else wrote this letter to Rafiq, not the Brilliant Trust. This also means that the person who has done this was aware that the Brilliant Trust didn't reply to Rafiq in two weeks and so he then wrote the letter. He must be close to Rafiq or that Rafiq was informing him about the progress of his scholarship application every few days,' he said. 'Maybe you can go to the address of the sender. However, I think it is a fake address. The person who has done it is very smart, I am sure,' suggested Seyyid. 'Maybe you can see the post office from where this was mailed and then see whose house is closer. But I still think that the person who has done this must have gone to a remote area and mailed the letter,' Seyyid concluded. Everyone was surprised at Seyyid's analysis and impressed by his interpretation and the ideas he had put forth. Rafiq's father requested everyone to recite a *salawat* for that person. Seyyid requested everyone to pray for such a noble person.

Qamar was away on a business trip abroad for the last few weeks. He returned and on Saturday, he went to Seyyid's house before *maghrib* and sat with him. He told him about his new business responsibilities after his father passed away and sought Seyyid's advice. Although he was in touch with Seyyid via his mobile but seeing him was a pleasure and brought serenity to his heart. He used to tell his friends, 'Seyyid has antidepressant effect on me.' He requested Seyyid to pray for him that the wealth he has inherited from his father doesn't affect his heart and take him towards worldly attraction and extravagance. Seyyid told him to have a simple life style and always spend more in the way of God and helping people. 'Give more *sadaqa*, hidden, without informing anyone. *Insha'Allah* you will be safe,' said Seyyid. After that Seyyid informed him about Rafiq's scholarship and the unknown sponsor. Qamar told Seyyid that he was aware of it as Rafiq is in touch with him and also others. 'Do you have any guess, who could have done this good action?' asked Seyyid while looking at his face. Qamar replied confidently: 'Seyyid you know very well that after my father's death, may God bless him, I have been irregular in my attendance to your lectures and have been rarely in touch with any friends. We are only connected via mobile.' But Seyyid inquired again: 'So you are not the person who is supporting Rafiq's studies, right?' Qamar replied: 'Esteemed Seyyid, I was not even in the country when someone wrote that letter to Rafiq. How can I be present here and there at the same time?' Seyyid then realized that Qamar is smart in responding and so he didn't ask any further questions. He only smiled and then said that this person seems to be very close to Rafiq. 'May God bless him and protect his good deed and make him one of the *abrar*,' he prayed. Qamar's face was expressionless and he also prayed with Seyyid.

Laptop

It was almost the time for *zuhr* prayers and everyone was getting ready with their *wuzu*. Today was a busy day at Seyyid's house and a lot of people had come, most probably because it was a public holiday. Suddenly a loud sound was heard in Seyyid's yard and everyone looked in that direction to see what had happened. Someone's backpack had dropped from the top of the big shelves and the student to whom it belonged then rushed to see if everything inside was intact. People were busy in *wuzu* and setting the carpet for prayers and no one paid any attention. However, the student's face showed that his laptop was badly damaged.

Soon afterwards, someone started saying *adhan* and then Seyyid came out of his room and said *iqamah* and then they had their prayers together. After prayers, Seyyid brought some sweets and then started his lecture on *tafakkur*, or contemplation. He said that in Islamic traditions, contemplation is regarded as a very valuable worship. It is said that an hour of contemplation is equal to sixty years of worship or even more. Then he explained the reasons for it, saying that contemplation actually changes the intentions behind our deeds. It also stops a person from doing a bad deed and also good deeds which are not done for the sake of God. He emphasized that even in the busy life of a big city, one should have a fixed time every day to do *tafakkur* for a few minutes. It is necessary because all of us are exposed to several diverse things, we meet so many people and see so many ugly things that without *tafakkur*, it is not possible for us to follow straight path and keep our minds clear and focused. *Tafakkur* serves as a scan disc for ourselves and lets us evaluate each and every of our intention and action and seek forgiveness from God. *Tafakkur* can also help a student to study harder and better without any distractions because it acts as a filter to clean the mind from distracting ideas and helps the brain function optimally with a noble aim every day. This is necessary for studies. Everyone was listening to his lecture with utmost attention…

After the lecture was over, people started saying goodbye to Seyyid. Seyyid noticed that the student by the name of Abid whose laptop had broken earlier was a bit uncomfortable. He asked Abid the reason. He told Seyyid that his laptop was badly damaged. 'I will take it to a shop to see if the data is recoverable or not. But the laptop screen is just dark. It doesn't work,' Abid said. Seyyid asked Abid to inform him if he needed any help.

Next day, Abid went to the computer shop and urgently wanted the engineer to check if it was reparable, and if not, inquire about the data recovery process. After few minutes, the engineer said: 'Your laptop is severely damaged and fixing it is impossible. This laptop model is a very old one. Even if I want to fix it, the parts are not available in the market.' 'I have exams in four weeks. Can you recover the data as soon as possible?' The engineer said that the data recovery will take two days. 'You should pay in advance for the hard drive I will use for data transfer,' he said. Abid agreed and informed his father about it. He then left for university on his bike. He dropped by Seyyid's house for *maghrib* but didn't stay for his lecture. After prayers, he just said Salams to a few students and friends and then left to go back to a library for studying and then went home late in the night. His mother opened the door for him.

'There is a box in your room. It came near *maghrib*,' said his mother. 'Okay mother, I will look at it. I am hungry now, have to eat something.' His mother then went to the kitchen to get some food ready for him. Abid went to his room, changed his clothes and casually looked at the box lying on his study table. It was a shock for him. It was a laptop box. At first, he thought it was his own laptop returned by the computer shop and the engineer probably was not able to recover his data. But this box was new. He quickly opened the box. There was an envelope pasted on the box. He opened the envelope and it had a typewritten message 'Gift from your friend, Seyyid.' In a state of surprise, Abid opened the box and found a brand new laptop from one of the best manufacturing companies of the world. The hard drive, RAM and other specifications were all very good; it probably was one of the best models available in the market.

He immediately ran to his mother and informed her. She came to his room and was surprised, as well as happy. 'Probably someone close to you, who knows that your laptop was damaged yesterday, has sent it,' she suggested. 'It is from Seyyid, mother, look at this message inside the envelope,' he suggested. His mother saw it and said that she was sure that it was not from Seyyid because he would never write his name on it. 'Okay, now you thank God for it and take your dinner. Leave the rest for tomorrow.' Abid turned on the laptop and then went to the kitchen for dinner. He then offered two *rak'ats* of prayers thanking God and also prayed for the person who had sent this gift in a timely manner. He looked at the box to find the shop address and noted it down so that he could find the person who had purchased it.

That night Abid while on his bed for sleep recalled how he met Seyyid for the first time through a friend two year ago. He had a problem in differentiating evolution and creation of God and so his friend took him to Seyyid's house at *zuhr* prayers. After prayers his friend introduced Abid and said that he has a question. Seyyid looked towards Abid with a smile. 'Respected Seyyid I have a problem in understanding evolution. Did it really happen? If not how can we prove the creation of animals and plants and this whole universe in a scientific way and also answer the questions posed by modern science?, he asked. Seyyid smiled and said: 'This is not so difficult. If a person gets lost in argumentation and discussions to find a scientific reason for every phenomenon, he will never find a clear and final answer because with progress of technology, a new reason or mechanism will be found for everything we see in this universe. However, you can very easily find clear answers of all your questions and defend yourself in discussions if you read *Hadithe Halila* or the 'Tradition of Myrobalan Fruit' of Imam Sadiq (as) for understanding the creation and proof of God and '*Hadithe Mufaddal'* of Imam Sadiq (as) for understating the divine wisdom of the creation of human beings, animals, plants and also natural events.' Abid thanked Seyyid and noted the names of these books. He purchased them and also found them online. Once he read these two books, he found all the answers. He then came to Seyyid, thanked him and gradually started attending his lectures.

Next day, Abid, with the laptop inside the box, went to the shop from where it was purchased. It was a big shop with lots of laptops on display and there were many customers. Abid went to the cashier and asked him about this laptop. The cashier checked in his computer and said that it had been purchased the day before, in the afternoon. 'Can I know the name of the person who paid for it, or his contact number?' 'Yes, why not.' Then the cashier gave Abid the name and contact number that was in his system. 'Do you remember his face?' Abid asked curiously. 'Excuse me sir, this is a busy shop and we have over 200 customers every day. I don't remember the face. By the way, that customer paid in cash, otherwise I could have given you his bank account number,' he said. Abid thanked him and left the shop and called the mobile number. It was out of service. He had reached a dead end….

He then went to Seyyid's house. It was before *zuhr* prayers. Seyyid welcomed him. When he saw Abid with the laptop box, he smiled. Abid told Seyyid what had happened the night before and in the morning. Seyyid listened patiently and then said that someone close to him who knew that his laptop was damaged has done it. Abid asked: 'Seyyid, I am sorry to ask, but the message I showed you has your name.' Seyyid smiled and looked at him and said: 'Abid, *mashaAllah* you are intelligent. How can I give a gift to you like that and then write my name on it?' Abid was ashamed. 'I am sorry Seyyid.'

Then Seyyid thoughtfully said: 'Someone who is very smart and was watching you very closely has done this nice good deed to please God and keep it a secret. Yesterday, many students and other people were here and they probably saw that your laptop was broken. Someone who also knew that your exams are near and that you need laptop urgently has done this.' Abid said that almost all the students here knew that I have my exams in a month. Seyyid then told him to pray for that person and also said that he should forget it. That person will never be known. 'Go home and seriously prepare for your exams and also pray to God to bless you with knowledge whenever you open your book to study.' Abid thanked Seyyid and left.

On Saturday, after *maghrib* prayers, Seyyid gave a lecture on *hasad*, or jealousy and how it destroys one's faith and good deeds. He explained that a jealous person is psychologically sick because instead of being happy and appreciative of others' talents and abilities, he feels stressed and threatened and tries to harm that person. He also mentioned in great detail signs and symptoms of jealousy – both in jealous person's intentions and thoughts as well as his behavior.

He also described in detail how jealousy leads to other moral problems and ugly sins such as hypocrisy, backbiting, insulting behavior, usurping their rights, physically harming the person towards whom one is jealous and even murdering him, etc. He then talked about methods to diagnose jealousy by a simple checklist. He said that a jealous person is psychologically sick person suffering from chronic stress and even intellectually abnormal because he makes incorrect judgements about those towards him he feels jealous.

He then mentioned the treatment of jealousy and that was to praise the person towards whom one feels jealous. 'Speak good about him behind his back, praise his good qualities that you don't have, give him a gift, and try to internally convince your heart that all the talents a person has are because God has blessed him. The abilities that you don't have but another person has, are because God has favored him. He doesn't have anything from himself. You should then pray God to bless you with those qualities and talent. If God wishes, He will bless you, otherwise He is All Wise and All Knowing to make the best judgement for you', he explained. Everybody was quietly listening to Seyyid's captivating words of practical wisdom. Some of them were concerned about themselves and doubtful if God forbid they had jealousy and looked towards each other in surprise.

After his lecture, Seyyid told everyone about Abid's new laptop and said that someone has put his name to cover up his good deed. 'Though this deed is praiseworthy, but the person who has done it should not have put my name on it.' He said.

Someone from the audience said to Seyyid that today's young people are so smart, especially when he has trained them so well. They want to do good deeds for the sake of God only and so the person perhaps wanted to make sure that Abid will not give the gift back to the shopkeeper and that's why he put Seyyid's name for easy acceptance by Abid and make him happy at that time of stress that he was going through. Seyyid smiled and said: 'Yes, the young generation is really very smart, much smarter than us, the older generation.' Everybody laughed at Seyyid's expression. Seyyid then prayed for that person and asked everyone to recite a *salawat* for him.

When everybody left, Seyyid told Abid that he should offer two *rak'at* prayers for the person who has given this precious gift to him in a timely manner, give *sadaqa* for his safety and good health and always try to remember him in his prayers.

Professional Career

'Respected Seyyid, thanks for everything you have done for my marriage arrangement. We will come in time *insha'Allah* before *maghrib*. My family will take care of necessary work for today's ceremony. I have also requested friends to be here before time. You have already done a lot and I will not be happy if you are troubled more than this,' said Husayn. Seyyid as usual smiled. 'You should leave now for preparations,' he said. Husayn said goodbye and left.

Husayn was getting married to Shareef's sister, Amina. Both had become doctors and it was Seyyid who had made the choice and proposed from both the sides and united the families. They were very happy with the way Seyyid set the scene for them and proceeded with marriage proposal. Seyyid's wife was equally involved in it. Husayn's mother was very happy and thanked Seyyid as he fulfilled his promise of finding a suitable bride for Husayn. Shareef's family was very well-educated and all his brothers and sisters were brought up to be very well mannered and religious. Seyyid specially wanted both of them to serve the society in the best possible manner as doctors.

At *maghrib*, all were present and in Seyyid's home yard the seats were arranged for the guests. After prayers, Seyyid informed everyone that today we will have a short regular lecture on *nifaq* or hypocrisy and then, we will have *nikah* with a short talk on the life of Imam Ali (as) and Hazrat Fatima (sa) and then dinner will be served.

In his lecture, Seyyid explained the two basic types of hypocrisy, verbal and behavioral. He also talked briefly about its signs and devastating effects on a person. 'Usually, a hypocrite has very high social and verbal communication skills. This is because he is an intelligent liar and adapts himself behaviorally with the environment and people against whom he practices hypocrisy. One can fall into the trap of a hypocrite easily. An intelligent *momin* should analyze the difference between words and actions of a person to detect hypocrisy,' he said. He ended his lecture with the hadith of prophet (swas): 'Three signs when found in anyone makes him a hypocrite even though he fasts and offers prayers and thinks that he is a Muslim: When he is trusted, he is dishonest, when he talks, he lies, and when he makes a promise, he breaks it.' He then prayed to God to bless them with an insight of ourselves and protect us from this deadly disease.

After that, he gave a short talk on husband and wife relations and presented Imam Ali (as) and Hazrat Fatima (sa) as perfect role models. He emphasized: 'This relationship is based on respect, care and mutual understanding and keeping in sight the aims of family life according to the divine view. This becomes more important in the time of difficulty and stress. The reason for so many problems with marriage in Western society is because marriage has lost its divine aspect and husband and wife behave as partners and friends and not as believers, parents, helpers of each other for a divine cause and for worshipping God and for serving society. Training well-mannered children and imparting knowledge to them and providing them with good education is a great service to society.' After that, he recited the *nikah* and then prayed for the new family and then they had food together. Finally, everyone left and at the end Husayn's and Shareef's families thanked Seyyid and they left too. Seyyid thanked God for yet another blessing.

After a few weeks, Husayn called Seyyid and requested his permission for a short meeting. 'My wife and I want your advice on an important matter which is related to our professional careers,' said Husayn. Seyyid asked him to come at 3 pm, when no one was usually present in the yard of the house. They arrived with some sweets for Seyyid and then

Husayn said: 'Respected Seyyid, as you know me and Amina want to specialize in surgery so that we can treat wounded patients. We are almost ready for residency entrance exam for going to USA. However, due to current situation of the region, we want to serve the poor and displaced people living in refugee camps for a year and then go to USA. After five years, we will return and serve our own society as you have taught us. During this one year, it will be possible for us to come here for a few days every four months and then go back.' Seyyid listened attentively and then said: 'God bless you. The plan seems good. You can even go now for your surgery specialization and then go to the hospitals in refugee camps to serve the displaced people.'

Husayn said that he and his wife wanted to taste the difficulty of serving in refugee camps at the prime of their specialization career so that they would always remember it. Seyyid smiled: 'So you want to have a memorable experience. Will your family allow both of you to go like that?' Husayn and Amina said that the difficulty lies here. 'We don't want to inform anyone about it. We can give our residency entrance exam, get the admission and visa and then go to serve the poor people for one year and then start training. So if someone asks us where are going, we can say that we are leaving for USA for specialization,' said Amina. Seyyid smiled and said: 'No, don't do that because if your families come to know of it, they will be unhappy. But you can hide it from other people. Don't worry, I will talk to your parents and get their approval, *Insha'Allah*.' They both agreed to keep it a secret and thanked Seyyid and then left.

Seyyid then made a few phone calls to the parents of Husayn and Amina. They also came to see him.

Husayn and Amina got busy with exam preparations and getting their paper work done for serving in the refugee camps through an international NGO. Few days later, Husayn and Amina got a phone call from Seyyid. After salams he asked both of them to come to his house and informed them that their parents were also coming. Both Husayn and Amina had fears that their parents were probably not happy with their plan....

They all met at Seyyid's house and then Seyyid and his wife served them with tea and snacks. Finally, Seyyid gave a surprise to Husayn and Amina: 'So both of you thought that your parents will not approve of your secret plan. In fact, they were very happy that *mashaAllah*, their kids have such high ambitions to serve the poor and displaced people, most of whom are women and children. I was also impressed by your parents for their approval. May Allah bless all of you.' The parents thanked Seyyid, Husayn's mother particularly thanked Seyyid for his education and training to all of them that changed their lives and also the lives of their kids. 'It's all your training Seyyid, otherwise we all know this was not possible,' she said. Seyyid immediately showed his slight displeasure and said: 'It's all God's grace upon us. He provides us both with opportunity and strength. We are nothing.' Finally, with the prayers of Seyyid they got up to leave. Husayn said to Seyyid that he will come with Amina to see him before leaving.

It was close to *maghrib* time and Husayn and Amina came to meet Seyyid. Some other students were also sitting. Seyyid welcomed them. After a few minutes, Husayn said: 'Respected Seyyid *alhamdolillah*, we have passed our residency exams to specialize in surgery in USA and we are planning to leave for abroad *insha'Allah* tonight.' Seyyid was very happy to hear that. Everyone in the gathering thought that Husayn and his wife were leaving for USA. Seyyid then prayed for them. 'When will you come back?' Seyyid asked him. 'After about a year, during the break; if it was possible, we may even come after four or eight months. It depends on our situation and load of work,' replied Husayn. Seyyid smiled and prayed for them and asked them to give *sadaqa* before leaving. 'Keep me informed via mobile,' he said. After they left, Seyyid thanked God for another good work.

*****

After about one year....

Seyyid had invited all of his close students. There were about fifteen of them. Husayn and his wife had also come for a short break from their voluntary medical service to refugee camps and so they were also invited. It was a special gathering after *maghrib* and *'isha* prayers on Monday when others had left. Seyyid first offered them a dinner. After that, they all sat on chairs in a circle in front of Seyyid. They then looked at Seyyid and wondered why he had invited them that evening…

Seyyid smiled at them and said that about a year ago, we talked about *birr* and *abrar*. 'At that time, I wished that some of those in the audience taste *birr* and become *abrar*. So as per my word, you are all invited today to answer the question: Did you taste the pleasure of *birr* or righteousness?'

All of them were quiet and expressionless. Some of them were looking at others if they would say something in response to Seyyid's question so that they don't have to say anything. However, no one said anything. They behaved as if this question doesn't concern them.... It was a total suspense and silence prevailed the gathering for over a minute. Nobody spoke.

Seyyid was looking at their faces… he was expecting an answer from at least one of them. But then he smiled… Among the students, in order to keep the respect of Seyyid, Qamar was bold enough to speak out on their behalf: 'Respected Seyyid, it seems that no one of us has done any good action that qualifies to be '*birr*'. The way you taught us how to achieve *birr* was probably out of our capacity. That's why we are all quiet.' They all agreed and most of them said: 'Yes Seyyid, this is true. Brother Qamar is right. We didn't do any good action like *birr…*'

Seyyid smiled and said: ‘However, it seems to me that all of you have done something to be qualified as *birr*. So let us share with each other so that we all learn better and newer ways to achieve *birr*. It will be itself a good deed. To share good action also has good reward.’

Everyone looked at Seyyid as if he was provoking them to speak out about their good deeds… Some of them smiled faintly to give a message to Seyyid that they will not be trapped…

Seyyid waited for a few seconds, looked at their faces one by one, but no one said anything. Then Asad said: ‘Respected Seyyid, even if a few of us have done some so called good action, it was done as a duty. So it doesn’t qualify as *birr*. Some of us may have done it only as a duty. May be some of us did it because we were forced to do it – we didn’t want to do good…’

Seyyid said: ‘Excellent. May God bless you all. You all are now *abrar*… because you have learned that keeping your good actions to yourself is the essence of a good action done purely for the sake of God. I tried to provoke you by saying that sharing good experience is a good deed but you didn’t fall in that trap. May God bless you all.

The beauty and the main attribute of *birr* action is that its pleasure remains fresh with that person and is always pleasurable. Every good action has a *thawab*, which is from the word *thawab*, meaning clean dress. Perhaps, it means that the reward or *thawab* of a *birr* action is such intense and powerful that the person feels it all the time in this world and it remains with him it like his clean dress.

Even if that person becomes old, blind, deaf and loses all his physical senses, the *birr* action remains with him like his clean dress. This is because it is related to the heart and spirit of that person and remains intact with him until the person dies.

After death the real *thawab* will be granted to him by God and its intensity and pleasure will be much more, may be thousand times more than pleasure of the physical world.

Every good action has its own specific pleasure that we cannot differentiate or perhaps weakly differentiate in this world with our physical senses. However, after death, when the divine vision will be bestowed, the pleasure of different *birr* actions will be felt separately. Holy Qur'an provides details of such pleasures in heaven.

Perhaps this is a window to heaven that believers feel this pleasure in this world and when they go to heaven they say that they have felt it before. It is also mentioned in the Qur'an. But remember that this good feeling and pleasure goes away or its intensity becomes less when a person talks about it for *riya*. Sometimes it is necessary to talk; but the style and expression should be such as to not to seek praise or thanks from the creatures of God.'

At that point, Asad asked a question from Seyyid: 'We know that every good action and bad action has an effect or reward and punishment. Qur'an says that even an atom's weight of good and bad action will be seen by the doer. So how will a *birr* action have a reward that can be seen by the doer? The reason is because it is hidden and not disclosed by him.' Seyyid smiled and said: 'The reward of any good or bad action starts right at that time when a person does it. But we don't see it with our physical eyes.'

'The reward of *birr* action is very powerful and affects the entire existence of the doer. Not only that, it affects his next generation and purifies and protects it from evil influences. The effects can be *barakah* (blessing) in his life, protection from diseases, opportunities for doing more good deeds, acquisition of worldly gains, respect in the hearts of good people, virtuous children and so on.

However, a true believer knows the effects of *birr*, but he never wishes anything from creatures. He only likes to serve God and seek His pleasure. This is the highest station. Imam Husayn (as) is the best example of such a high status. When Shimr wanted to sever his head on the day of Ashura, he heard Imam Husayn (as) whispering prayers to God: 'I am happy at Your decision and I have surrendered to Your order.' Thus Imam Husayn (as) did all the sacrifices only for the sake of God until the last moment of his life.' Everyone was moved by Seyyid's words... He continued: 'So now you all keep your good actions preserved for the hereafter and do not ruin them by doing *riya* or making show of it, even by your subtle gestures. May God bless you all.'

Seyyid ended his talk with a hadith from Prophet (swas) which said that a righteous action has three characteristics: it is done quickly, it is kept hidden and it is considered insignificant by the believer who does it. Then Seyyid gave each of them a gift, one by one they went near him and received it and Seyyid prayed for them. They all thanked Seyyid for his guidance, care, and training, putting them to test smartly and asked him to pray for them... They left one by one, saying goodbye to Seyyid.

A tragedy after about five years....

Seyyid continued his spiritual lectures and ethical training of young college and university students at his home. All the twelve students continued their careers keeping close contact with him. Some of them went abroad for pursuing their higher education, while others went to different cities. After about five years, few of them returned back to their home country and settled down with jobs in universities, different organizations and industries. Those who lived in the city, used to attend his lectures and often visited him for guidance. Few others who were still continuing their education, Seyyid was in touch with them via email while sometimes they would call Seyyid to talk to him and listen to his sweet and calming voice and get some advice.

It was afternoon one day before *zuhr* prayers when Seyyid was with his students and answering their questions about different issues. His mobile phone rang and the students saw that as soon as Seyyid picked the mobile and listened to the other side, a flare of sadness appeared on his face and then he said '*Inna lillah wa inna ilaihe rajeoon*' (*'*Indeed we belong to Allah and to Him do we indeed return*'*). After few minutes of listening to the other side, they heard Seyyid saying: "My dear Shareef be patient. I know you are very sad, I know it's difficult, but it has great reward from God. You must also take care of your parents, especially your mother. You must be satisfied with what God has destined and what a great felicity it is for both of them. You should be thanking God for this great blessing. When you feel comfortable come to me. We will have gathering here........ Yes, yes I will recite the funeral prayers. ..... Let the bodies arrive..... be patient my dear...God be with you...."

All the students including Qamar, Shahid and Asad were in a state of surprise and shock. They never saw Seyyid so sad. As soon as Seyyid hang up his phone, one of them asked, 'What happened dear Seyyid, who has passed away?' Seyyid replied: "Dr Husayn and his wife Dr Amina were martyred today morning in our neighbouring war torn country. A terrorist attack on their field hospital led to their martyrdom. A few others including nurses and health workers from other countries were also martyred and injured. After completing their medical specialization, instead of staying in western country and enjoying rich and peaceful life, Dr Husayn and Dr Amina had decided to voluntarily serve in the war torn country where millions of displaced oppressed children, weak, sick and women needed medical care. They were serving in a field hospital clinic for the last one year…… '

'But Seyyid, martyr Dr Husayn never told us about it, we were in touch with him and his wife, we thought they were still in the country where they completed their medical specialization…' interrupted Shahid.

Seyyid calmly replied: "Husayn and his wife never wanted anyone to know about it. They wanted to keep their services to oppressed, totally secret. After completing their medical education, they came back here for short time to meet their parents and they also met me. However, they never told anyone including their parents about their exact destination. After starting their work, they contacted them and regularly spoke to them giving impression of a happy, rich and peaceful life in a western country where they pursued their education. I also came to know through a friend who works with international humanitarian services. He accidently visited the field hospital where they were working as physicians few months ago. He gave me their phone numbers. When I asked them about their location and their plans to come back to our own country, they told me that they are practicing medicine and are happy, living in a peaceful place and they will come back soon. They didn't disclose their location, city or country."

Seyyid then asked to make preparations for *zuhr* and *'asr* prayers.

After they had *zuhr* and *'asr* prayers, Seyyid did *du'a* for martyred Dr Husayn and Dr Amina and for patience to their families. He then called their parents and consoled with them. He was requested to pray funeral prayers when their bodies will arrive in next one or two days. The students also started calling their close friends. Qamar, Shahid and Asad were very sad and they were discussing how to offer their support to the family of Dr Husayn and Dr Amina. They informed Sobhan, Bilal, Yusuf, Shareef, Ahmad, Mostafa, Ibrahim and Vaheed about this sad tragedy. They also called their own home and informed parents and other close relatives. Soon many of them were heading to the houses of parents these two martyrs.

After two days, their bodies arrived. By that time, the news of their humanitarian medical services and sacrifice were in media and so thousands gathered in the main city mosque for their funeral. Seyyid went with father of Dr Husayn from his home to recite funeral prayers. At the request of families, he also did the burial rituals himself for his two beloved students. Several scholars, intellectuals, and the university professors who were teachers of Dr Husyan and his wife also came to attend the funeral prayers. It was a very sad scene.

On the third day, Seyyid held a memorial ceremony at his own place to pay tribute to Dr Husayn and Dr Amina. Families and friends of these two martyrs were present. Other students of Seyyid who were in different cities also arrived. The courtyard of Seyyid's house was full. Those who knew the families of martyrs consoled with them. After *maghrib* and *'isha* prayers, Seyyid gave a very sad and inspirational lecture. Together with his spiritual words, it had special effect on the audience.

He began with the verse of Holy Qur'an:

وَلَا تَحْسَبَنَّ الَّذِينَ قُتِلُوا فِي سَبِيلِ اللَّهِ أَمْوَاتًا ۚ بَلْ أَحْيَاءٌ عِندَ رَبِّهِمْ يُرْزَقُونَ

Do not suppose those who were slain in the way of Allah to be dead; no, they are living and provided for near their Lord. [3: 169].

Then Seyyid started with the real meaning and status of martyrdom and its importance in Qur'an and Islamic traditions. He said that all the sins of martyrs are forgiven as soon as the first drop of their blood is shed on ground. He then said that it means, the moment of their martyrdom. He then explained their life in heavens and their sustenance from God. "Martyrs are blessed servants of God whom He chooses for Himself. There are different stations of martyrs in heavens. Among them, those who voluntarily make choice to die in the way of God by courageously putting their lives in danger have very high station in heavens because they detach themselves from all transient, material and worldly attachments while living in this world. They prepare themselves to leave this world before they physically depart from it. In this way, they have no death in real sense of word and so they are not dead. While they live in this world, they live like a passenger who will depart any moment. Thus, their souls have a divine flavor while they are living physically with their body. So in reality, their departure from this physical world is very pleasant for them, as if they fly straight to heavens within the wink of eye. The angels and those whom they love such as Ahlul Bayt (as), *awliya* and martyrs of their own station welcome them. Now, there, they have complete peace and serenity by the special grace of their Lord. Because in the transient world they obeyed command of their Lord and sold their souls for divine and eternal returns. For them, transient pleasures of world had no importance compared to the eternal promise of their Lord." Seyyid said. Everyone was absorbed in his inspirational words of praise about martyrs.

After a while, Seyyid praised Dr Husayn and Dr Amina as: "These two martyrs are role models for those students who are very talented and who go abroad to study and pursue highest level of education in their fields to become doctors, engineers, researchers, experts in social sciences, humanities and like. Then they have choice to have worldly life with wealth, fame, peace and prosperity. Many of them lose their traditional culture, style of living, religious values and adopt western lifestyle. Their next generation also loses these and becomes a part of the oppressive system and lose their hereafter. A few of them who opt to stay there struggle hard and keep their religious values and Islamic lifestyle and propagate their religion. They train their next generation with utmost care and healthy Islamic family lifestyle."

"Dr Husayn and Dr Amina had choice to live in the western country and have rich, peaceful, professional and family life, continue to live there as good believers and carry out their religious and social duties, help poor and needy, propagate their religion, impart knowledge to their students, train them to be good physicians and human beings. That was an exemplary and praiseworthy life in this world and as well as a blissful life well rewarded in hereafter. But they had much higher aim than it. Their souls were tender to feel pain of those who have no helper, no one to come their help, no one to listen to their cries for relief of their pain and their sickness. While these oppressed children and women and weak lived in refugee camps, their poor health because of unhealthy diet, lack of hygienic support, medicines and basic healthcare facilities, led to deaths from common diseases, malnutrition and infections. They also suffered from psychological problems as many of these were orphans and widows. They often suffered from war injuries and lacked medical facilities and specialist physicians. No expert physician from developed country enjoying peaceful life there would voluntarily dare to go to a war ridden country and risk his life to treat these patients while getting almost no salary for it. It requires a courageous heart, strong will and empathic spirit with love of oppressed to make such a choice and to go to dangerous place and be happy to serve. Dr Husayn and Dr Amina were gifted to serve there."

"Dr Husayn being a good surgeon and Dr Amina being a child specialist were able to treat most of the oppressed refugees living in camps. They had a team of few more physicians from other countries together with nurses and health care workers. They were also imparting basic education in make shift schools for the kids."

"Above all, the divine beauty of Dr Husayn and Dr Amina is their sincerity for the sake of love of God and pure service to humanity and that is they didn't inform anyone about their journey to that war ridden country and work in the field hospital near refugee camps to anyone – not even their parents. They didn't want any praise for their sincere service to God. Only I came to know about it few months ago and then I informed Shareef, Dr Amina's brother about it while taking promise to keep it a secret. Informing more people would have made them unhappy."

"Dr Husayn and Dr Amina have truly earned highest reward for their *birr* and they are really *abrar* as God has mentioned in the Holy Qur'an. They have fulfilled their promise they made with me and they have earned perfect marks in their test. They are now with their beloved in heavens and they are enjoying heavenly life. May God bless their respected parents who have educated them and given them good family environment and training that they were able to achieve such a high station. Every action they did goes back to their parents."

"I request all the good students here to follow example of martyrs Dr Husayn and Dr Amina and earn highest place for them in this world and in hereafter. Indeed for all of us, the inspiration for such lofty actions come from Imam Husayn (as) and his sincere companions in Karbala. They are the real source of martyrdom seeking courageous life against injustice."

"Please recite surah Fatiha and then *salawat* for these two great believers and members of our gathering. We will always remember them and they will also remember us from heavens. *InshaAllah*."

After lecture, dinner was served, Seyyid himself was serving food to guests with his close students. Everyone was sad and quiet. Some students and guests were going near to parents and relatives of Dr Husayn and Dr Amina and offering their condolence to them.

After most of the guests had left, parents and siblings of Dr Husayn and Dr Amina went near Seyyid and thanked him for all he had done to make his two students spiritually and ideologically strong over a period of several years when they attended his lectures and took guidance from him. Seyyid listened to them patiently without moving, looking down and kept quiet. "It was your training and guidance respected Seyyid. We just provided them means to be educated at school, college and university. You imparted real education to be lofty human beings and sincere believers and obedient servants of God. Their martyrdom is because of your mentoring, your own love and careful nurturing of high values. …" Seyyid said: "I have only done my duty. I have done nothing special. Both of them were *mashaAllah* very talented, very practical and exceptionally devoted students. May Allah bless all of you."

After that gradually they all left. Seyyid specially thanked fathers and mothers of these two martyrs. He said that every Friday morning he will visit their graves until the fortieth day of their martyrdom. He asked them to visit him and he would like to talk to them. They all thanked him and left.

That night Seyyid was in deep thought. He was awake whole night praying to God and reciting special prayers…..

Today, after twenty years....

Today was a huge gathering in a mosque near Seyyid's house. It was the 40th day after he passed away due to short illness. Several of his students, friends, relatives and those who used to attend his lectures had gathered from different cities and countries. They were all very sad and talking about him, his good lectures, his polite and compassionate behavior, his good actions and the role he had played in their lives. A local scholar, who was a friend of Seyyid, then gave a speech on Seyyid's life. The speech was a great shock for almost all of Seyyid's students and even close friends. They were weeping and missing him even more...It was a sad scene. Seyyid's story had captured their hearts.

The scholar started his speech with ayah of Qur'an and then said... 'Perhaps most of you know your teacher and mentor who used to live a very simple and seemingly closed life and give lectures at his house and help you all as 'Seyyid Baqir', the person you thought had probably received traditional religious education and that he was as such from the beginning of his professional career. It was not like that....'

'Your Seyyid was my close friend for the past 40 years. He belonged to a rich family. He was the top student in his high school, college and then in university. He then left for USA and studied in one of the best institutions there and got his PhD in applied ethics and psychology with flying colors. He then finished his post-doctoral training making new discoveries in that field and then became an assistant professor in another top university. All of his family members live there. A few of them are here with us after twenty years when they heard of his death. May God bless him.' Everybody recited *salawat* and voices of weeping and sighs could be heard in the hall…

He continued… 'At that stage of his career, he had all the opportunities to make a future for himself and his new family in the West. He was recently married at that time and had a daughter. He then started his research on a totally new topic in ethics and psychology and won a grant of several hundred thousand dollars. He was also a successful psychologist right from his early professional career and worked as a consultant earning a good amount of money. He had published few very good research papers at that time. His life and career were full of potential to grow and make him famous. Even I didn't know it until today when I met his brother after 25 years… He kept all his achievements a secret from me as well.' Sighs were now heard across the hall.

The scholar then continued… 'His brother told me yesterday that 'Seyyid' then suddenly felt that serving and making career in a Western society was a treachery to his own people. He was sad to see young people living in developing countries having no guidance about their career. He felt that it was necessary to make their lives and counter the wave of Western culture that was destroying their lives and distorting their ideology. He then resigned from the university and left with his family for Qom to study in a seminary for few years. Since he had learned Arabic before and his religious base was very strong from the beginning, he was able to get the permission to teach religious and ethical sciences within a few years. He then left for your city and settled down here without exactly informing about his profession to his own family members back in USA. I too thought that he left Western society only because of his own children. I didn't know that he had a noble aim in his life which he kept hidden. Please recite a *salawat* for his noble spirit.' The audience recited *salawat* in the midst of sighs and sobs.

'And now I have another surprise for you. The brother of 'Seyyid' has brought his few old pictures, valuable documents and certificates, shields and awards he received in USA and from his past life before that. Few others of these are taken with the permission of Seyyid's wife. Seyyid and his wife kept these valuable things here for the last 25 years hidden in their house. All these are now displayed in the yard of Seyyid's house where many of you used to attend his lectures during the last over twenty years. After my speech is over, we will go there to see the past of this great man – may Allah bless his soul. Please recite *salawat...*'

'And finally the last secret of this great man... You might be curious sometimes about the source of earning of Seyyid. Was he supported by his family? No. I also didn't know until yesterday when his wife disclosed that Seyyid used to run online courses on ethics, spirituality, and spiritual psychology and provided counselling to people. He kept the payment option open for his courses and counselling at his website and never forced anyone to pay. A lot of young people, especially university students benefitted from his online courses. However, he never disclosed his identity or home address and so nobody knew who was taking the courses. He was using a pseudonym of Dr. S.M. Sadiq. Perhaps some of you or your kids may have taken courses from the website psychology teacher online. Several patients suffering from psychological problems including depression, anxiety, stress and other such conditions used to benefit from his advices on daily basis through the website. This is yet another glorious aspect of Seyyid's life that he was financially independent and every day he spent about 5 to 6 hours online to take courses and provide psychology counselling services and earn a respected living. This also meant that all the lectures he gave and help that he provided to many of you was free and out of his pocket as a duty and obligation that he took upon himself several years ago when he came back to his country. What a great soul he was and what a successful life he had. May God bless him. Please recite *Surah Fatiha* for him.'

After the speech, the guests had food. Most of them were quiet and remembering the memorable life they had with Seyyid… His face, his polite manners and his words of guidance, moments he provided compassionate advices to his students and attendees of his lectures were now in front of their eyes. Many of them were still in a state of shock after knowing that Seyyid, besides having had an excellent career at a top university in the West as a brilliant psychologist and ethicist, had also successfully studied at a seminary. They all ate food quietly and were now eager to leave for his house…

Sobhan, Qamar, Asad, Bilal, Shahid, Yusuf, Shareef, Ahmad, Mostafa, Ibrahim and Vaheed were all together again after several years. Today they were missing Dr Husayn and his wife Dr Amina. While they all lived in different cities and most of them in the same city, and they were in touch with Seyyid, it was after several years that they were all there together with their family members. They were in their cars. Sobhan and Bilal told their family members that they had taken online courses with Dr. S.M. Sadiq a few years ago but didn't know that it was Seyyid who offered them. They all now reached Seyyid's house.

All of them and several others went inside and in the yard saw Seyyid's old pictures, his certificates, shields, awards, his books, his research articles and proof of his past achievements that were hidden from their lives. 'Look papa, Seyyid was also a great debater during his college life,' said Bilal's son. 'And he was a mountain climber too. Look at this photo,' said Bilal. They were explaining to their family members, especially their sons and daughters, about Seyyid's great life and his words of wisdom that had changed their own lives.

These students were now very sad, some had tears in their eyes and some were just shocked to see what a great intellectual

Seyyid was... They wished their own sons and daughters to follow his example. After a few minutes, they said good bye to Seyyid's brother and his two sons and came out of his house. While standing in the parking lot, they started exchanging last few words with each other before leaving for their homes...

Mostafa said: 'Brothers do you remember several years ago Seyyid gave few lectures on '*birr*' and qualities of '*abrar*?' Others recalled and everyone said that yes they remembered. Ahmad said that he had given a copy of important points to everyone. Then they recalled that a few years ago one of the attendees of Seyyid's lectures came with his friend from USA. His friend wanted to take Seyyid's advice about his personal matters. He asked questions to Seyyid in English. 'Do you recall that Seyyid spoke excellent and fluent English with that person and replied to all of his questions?' said Asad. 'I was surprised at that time and asked him after the guests had left about where he had learned English.' Mostafa continued. 'Seyyid was so smart. He smiled and replied to me "I learned English when I was in school and I am not an expert in English language".' 'Of course, a true believer is smart,' said Qamar. 'And his wife too! I am his son-in-law for the last 14 years and I never saw them talking in English or giving an impression that they have lived in the West before,' said Shareef. 'Truly amazing,' said Vaheed. 'They are really great people.'

Ibrahim said: 'Alas, we didn't know that our dear Seyyid and his wife are too of the '*abrar*'. His station is much higher than all of his students and others to whom he practically taught how to achieve '*birr*'. Our martyred brother Dr Husayn and his wife Dr Amina are the best examples of his trained students. Husayn and his martyred wife never informed us that they were going to serve oppressed people of war-torn country after completing their medical education. Our Seyyid's station is certainly much higher than his trained students. He never spoke about himself. He achieved it with his piety, worship and knowledge. He was truly a great man, close to God.' All of them were sad and quiet for few moments...

Ibrahim asked: ‘So brothers, did anyone of you perform an action of ‘*birr*’ in your lives?’ And everyone said a loud ‘No’. They all smiled and said goodbye to each other.

Seyyid was alive in their hearts and their lives….

THE END

www.ingramcontent.com/pod-product-compliance
Lightning Source LLC
LaVergne TN
LVHW020642100826
845148LV00012B/2300

9781733028400